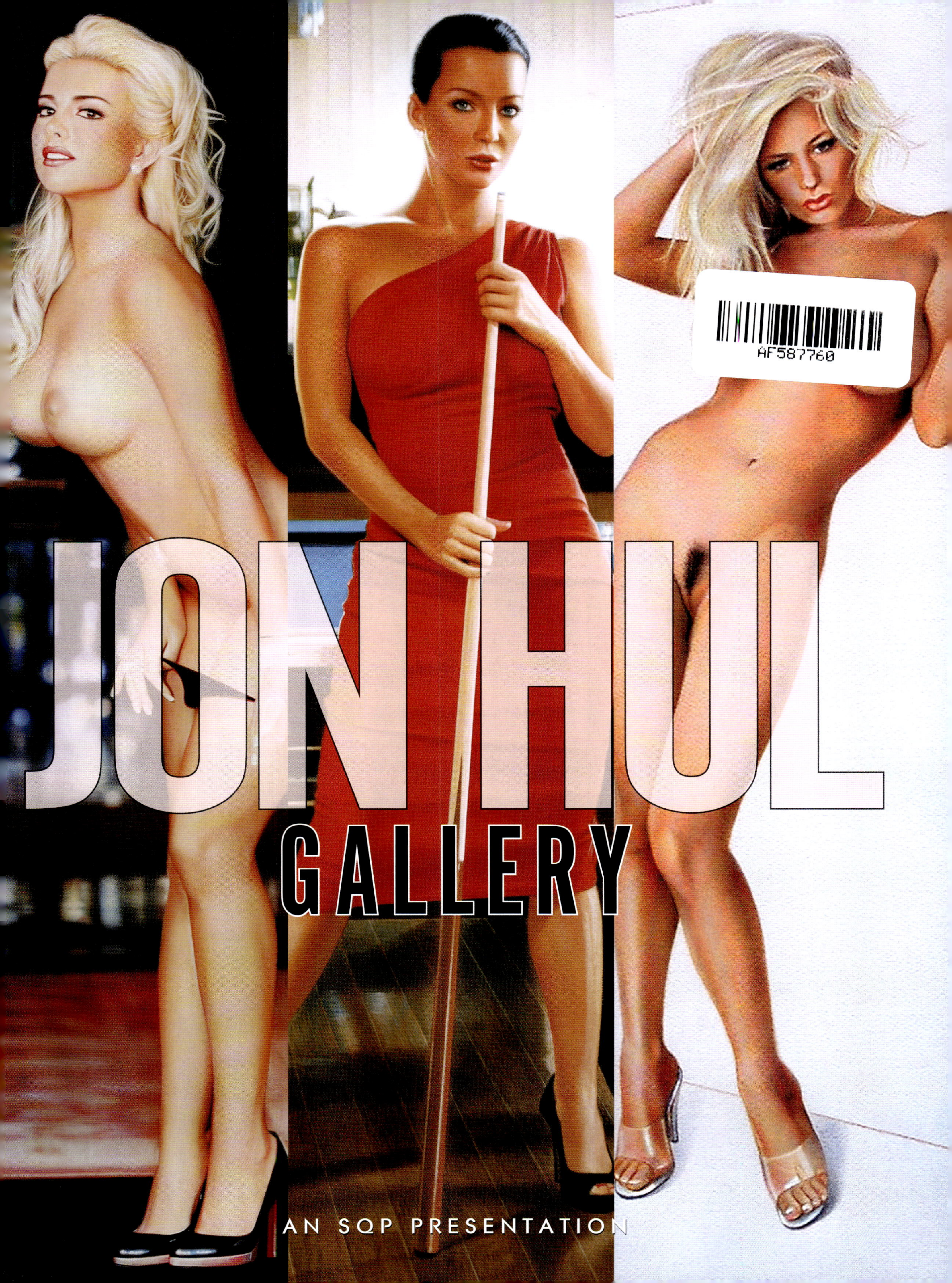
JON HUL
GALLERY
AN SQP PRESENTATION

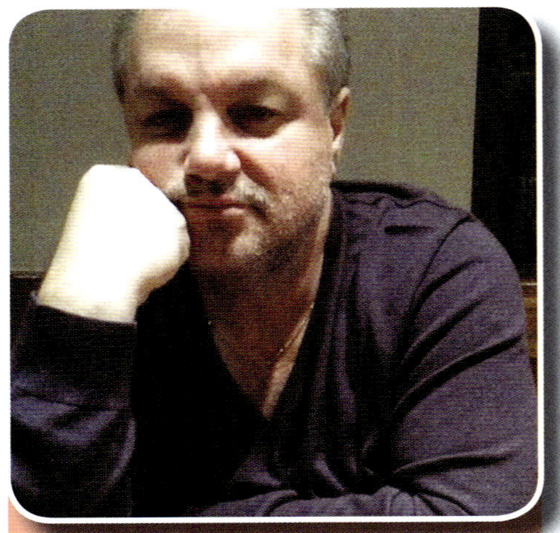

Rendering the most beautiful creatures in the world...women!!

Most women love creative men. (Speaking as an artist) I think women feel there is a certain "romantic" element within a man who can express himself, artistically. The idea of someone being special in that way- unique and deep. I'm certain that women tend to be more about emotional expression, as well as the aesthetics, as well as enjoying music, too. A good combination! It's quite possible that some women think that a man who is artistic or musically gifted will also apply those sides of himself into a relationship.

Throughout the years, as an established artist, I like expressing my art talent within the genre of art I render. I had no idea it was even possible to be passionate (as much as I am) about what I do. The feeling gets stronger as years pass. My constant thought process and approach in the way I render art of women delves into my passionate side... it's what motivates me. Plus, I get inspiration from friends, models, people I have met along the way in my art career, as well. The things I see and/or do everyday, and think I can eventually apply it in my work, as I do.

My ideas, dreams and goals are everlasting... As I shall prevail again and again in more of my works, in years to come!

Jon Hul
peace

Acknowledgements:
Jon Hul would like to acknowledge and thank his book publisher - SQP Art Books - Sal Quartuccio, and Bob Keenan.

A very special thank you to my beautiful wife- Terina! I am forever grateful of her undying support and belief in my art talent! She is the one most responsible in helping me make this book project, possible! We share a immense love & common bond with each other for more than 28 years!

Eggy
oxox

MODEL BEHAVIOR AND MUSE MANAGEMENT

Thanking the ladies who participated in making this book possible:

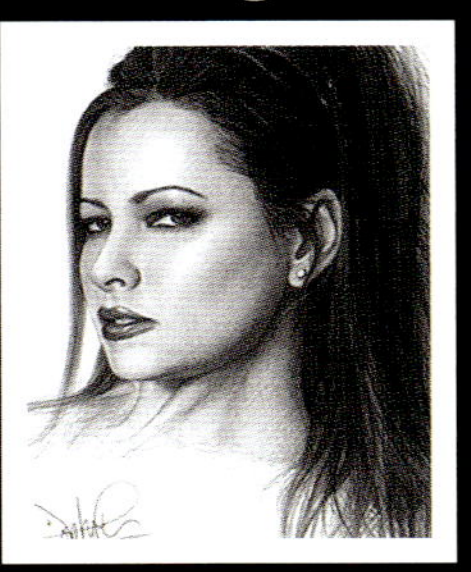

Angela Melini

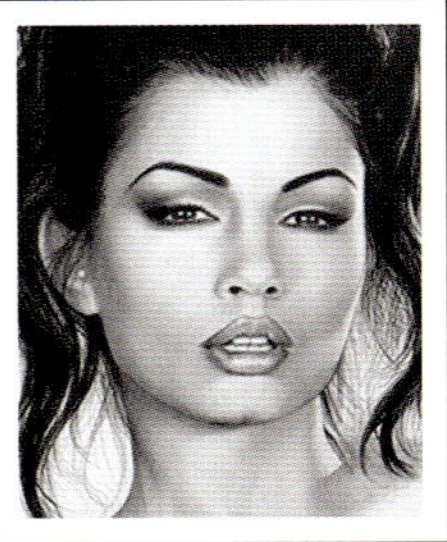

Aria Giovanni

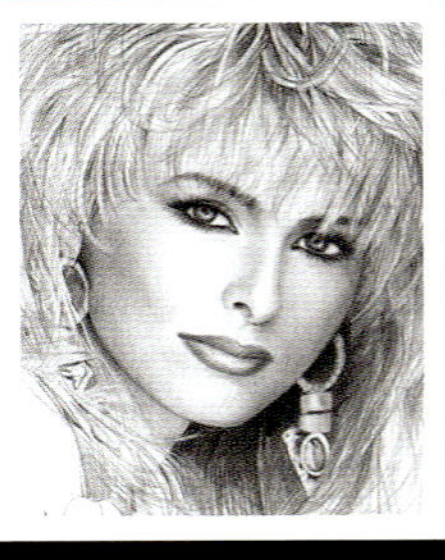

Cathy St. George

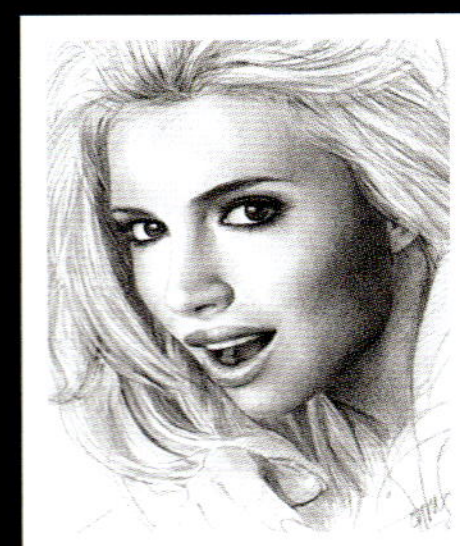

Destiny Davis

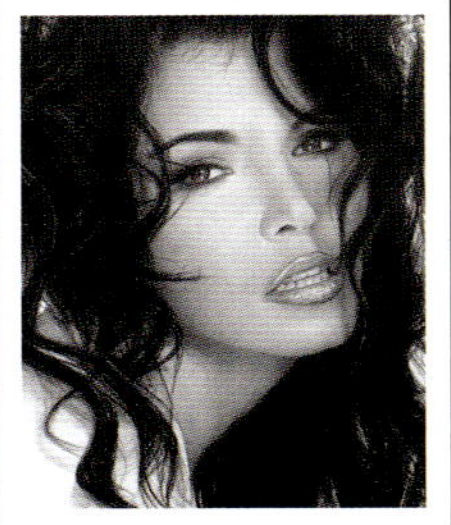

Devin DeVasquez

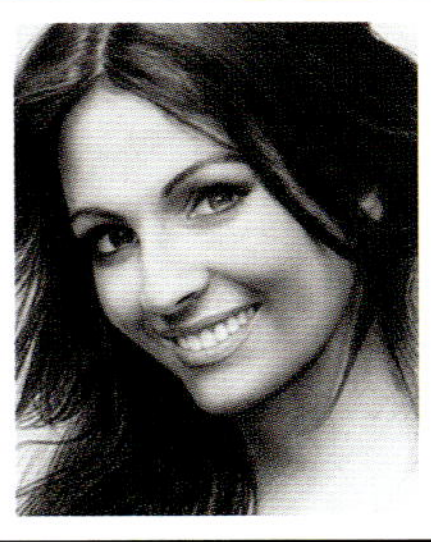

Denise Milani

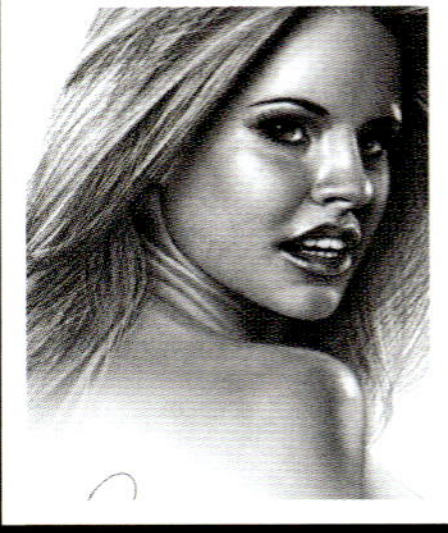

Jade Rieger

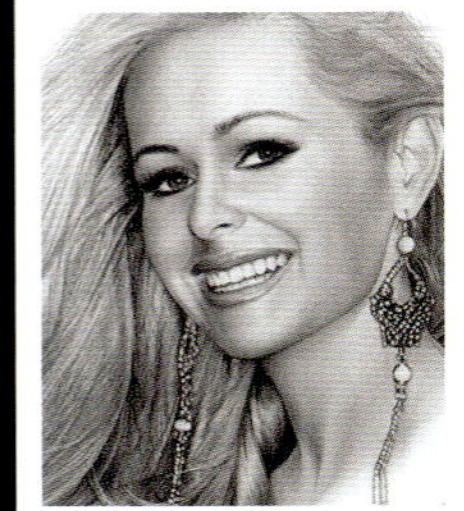

Katie Lohmann

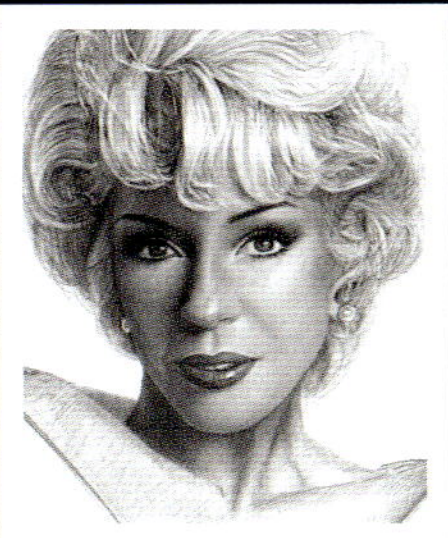

Kay O'Hara

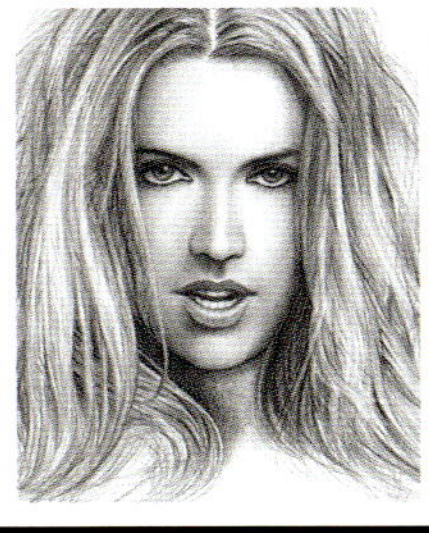

Leslie Sanchez

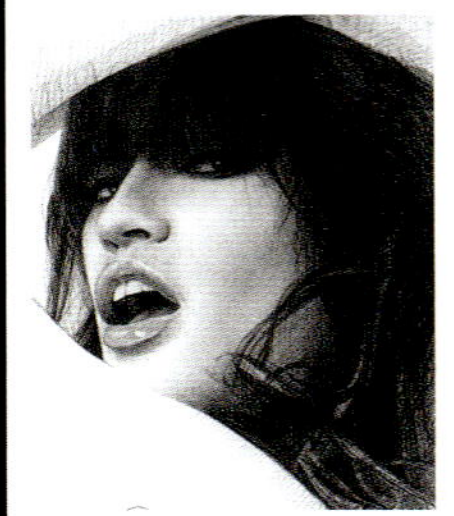

Lisa Boyle

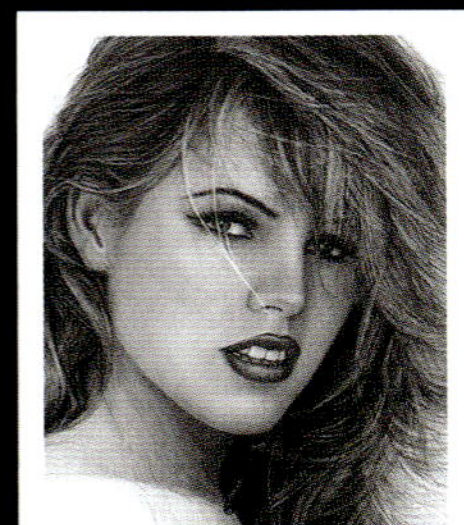

Sandra Taylor

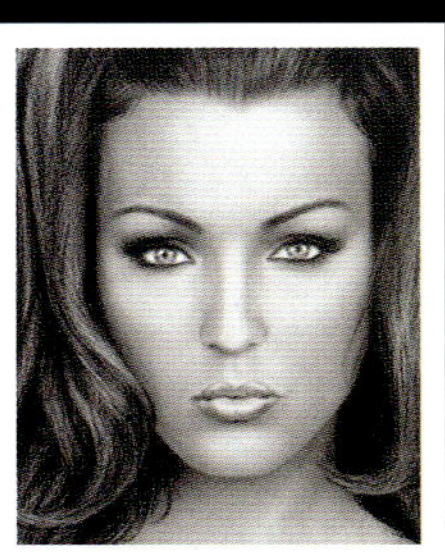

Shannon Stewart

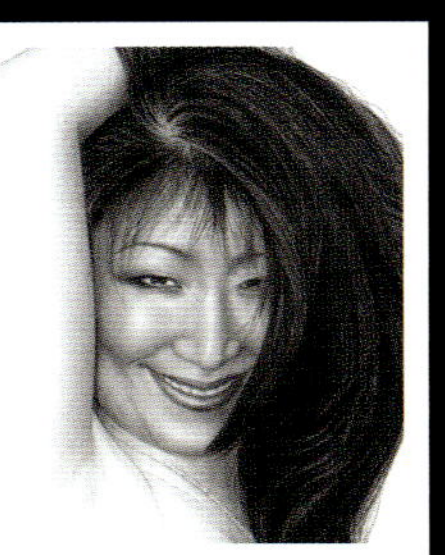

Terina Hul

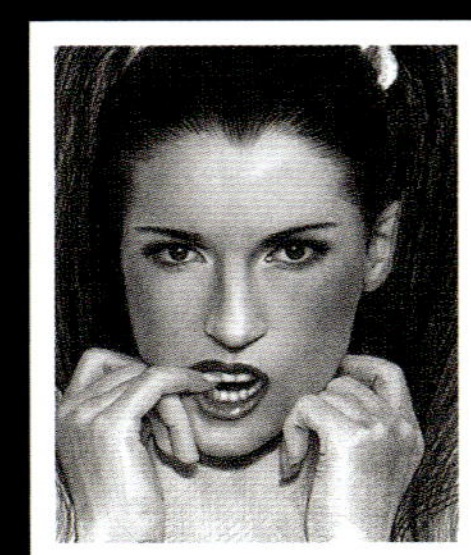

Tylyn John

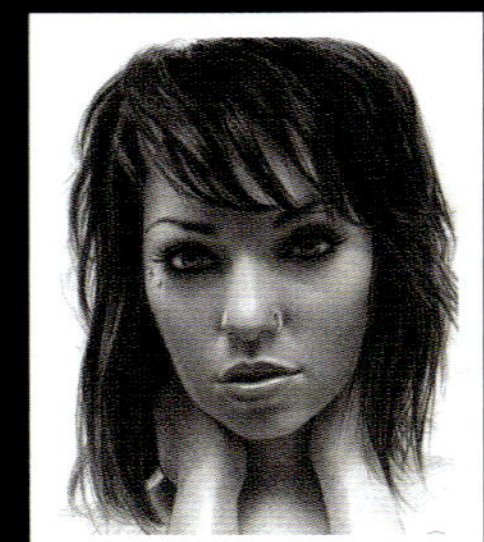

Jessica Goodwin

Jon Hul Gallery

Book design by Grassy Knoll Studios.

Published by SQP Inc.
PO Box 248 - Columbus NJ 08022
Sal Quartuccio & Bob Keenan - Publishers

For a free, full color catalog showcasing the entire SQP line of erotic, fantasy, and pin-up artwork, go to:
www.sqpartbooks.com

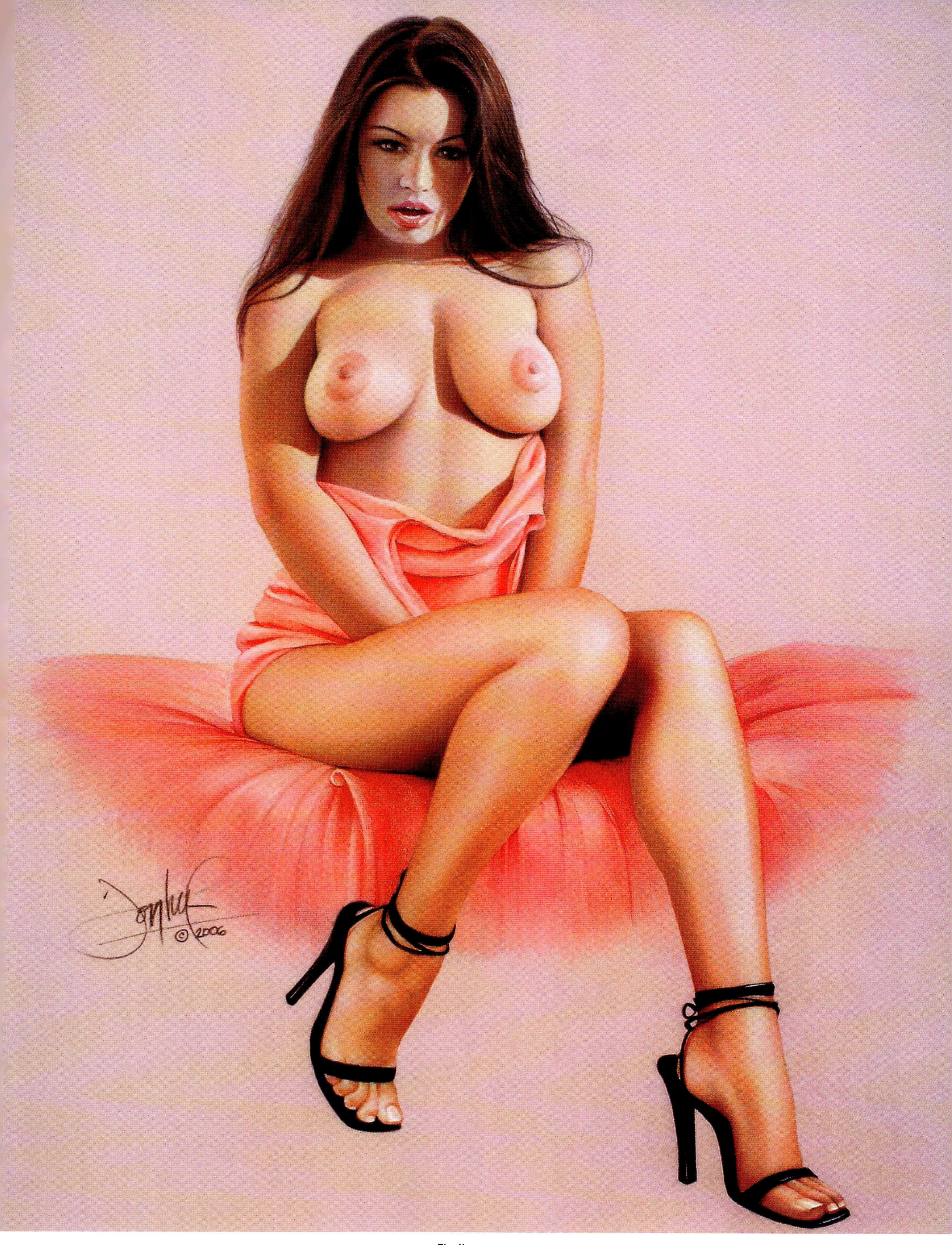

The Urge

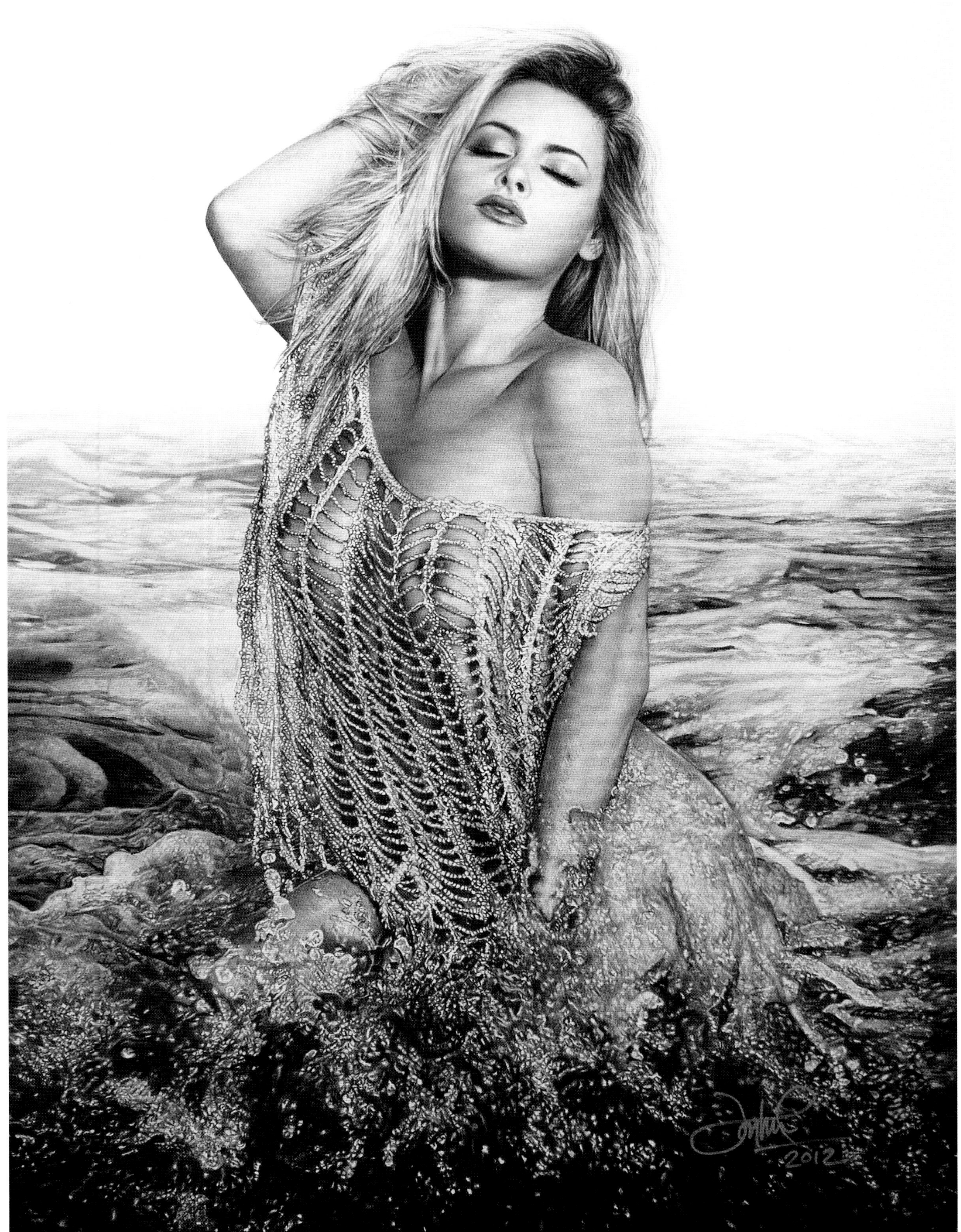

Untitled

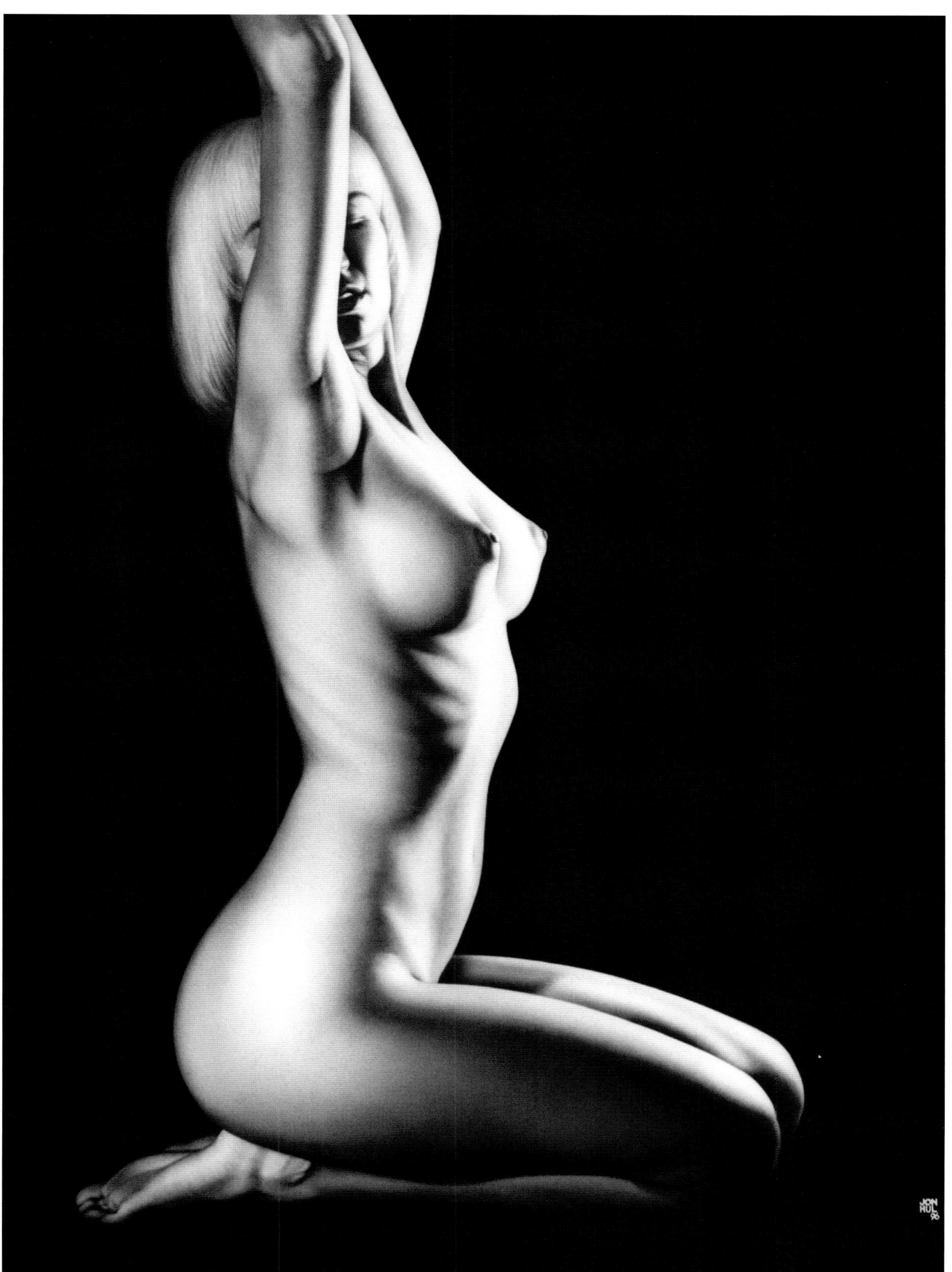

Tranquility

jon hul
2011

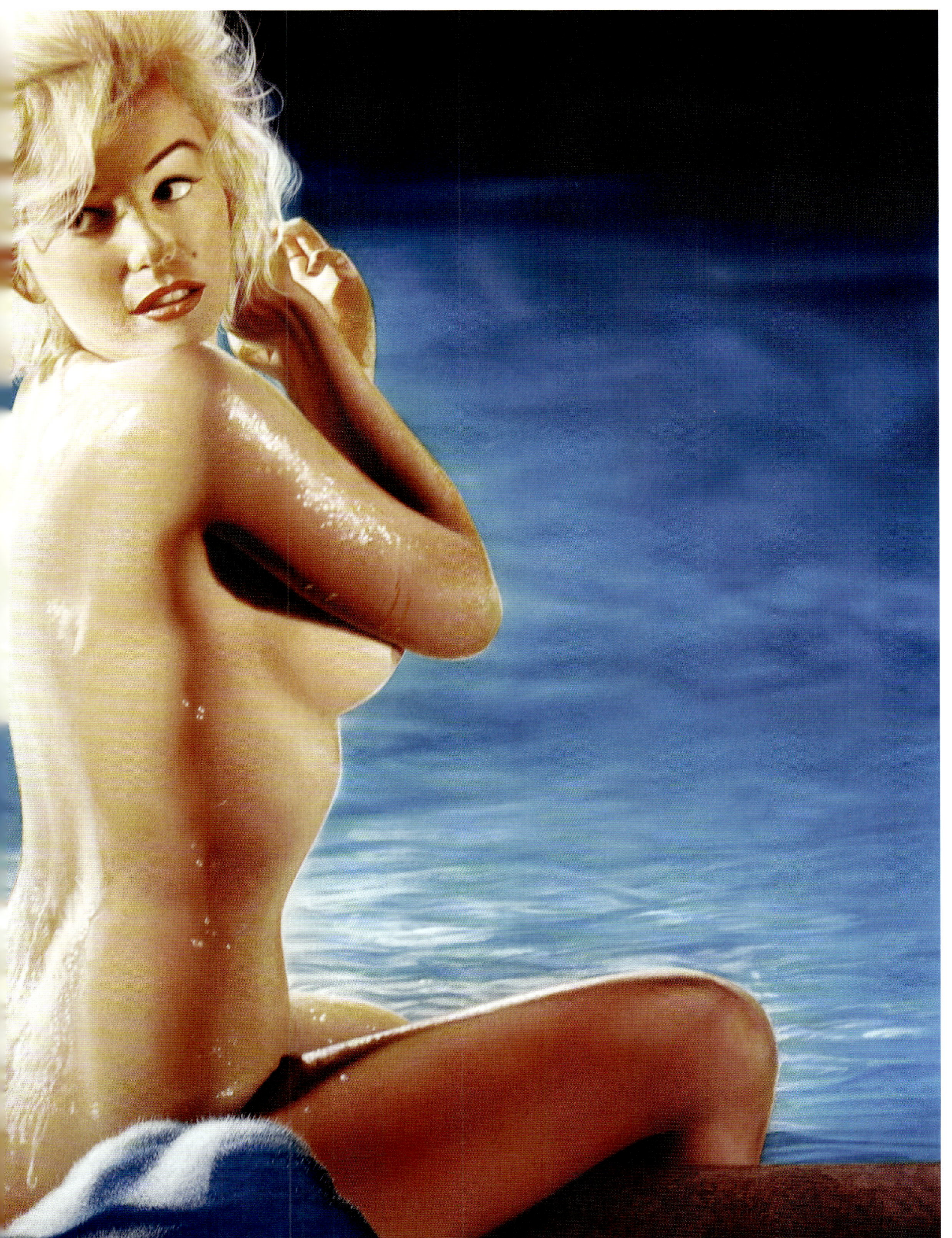

Something to Always Give

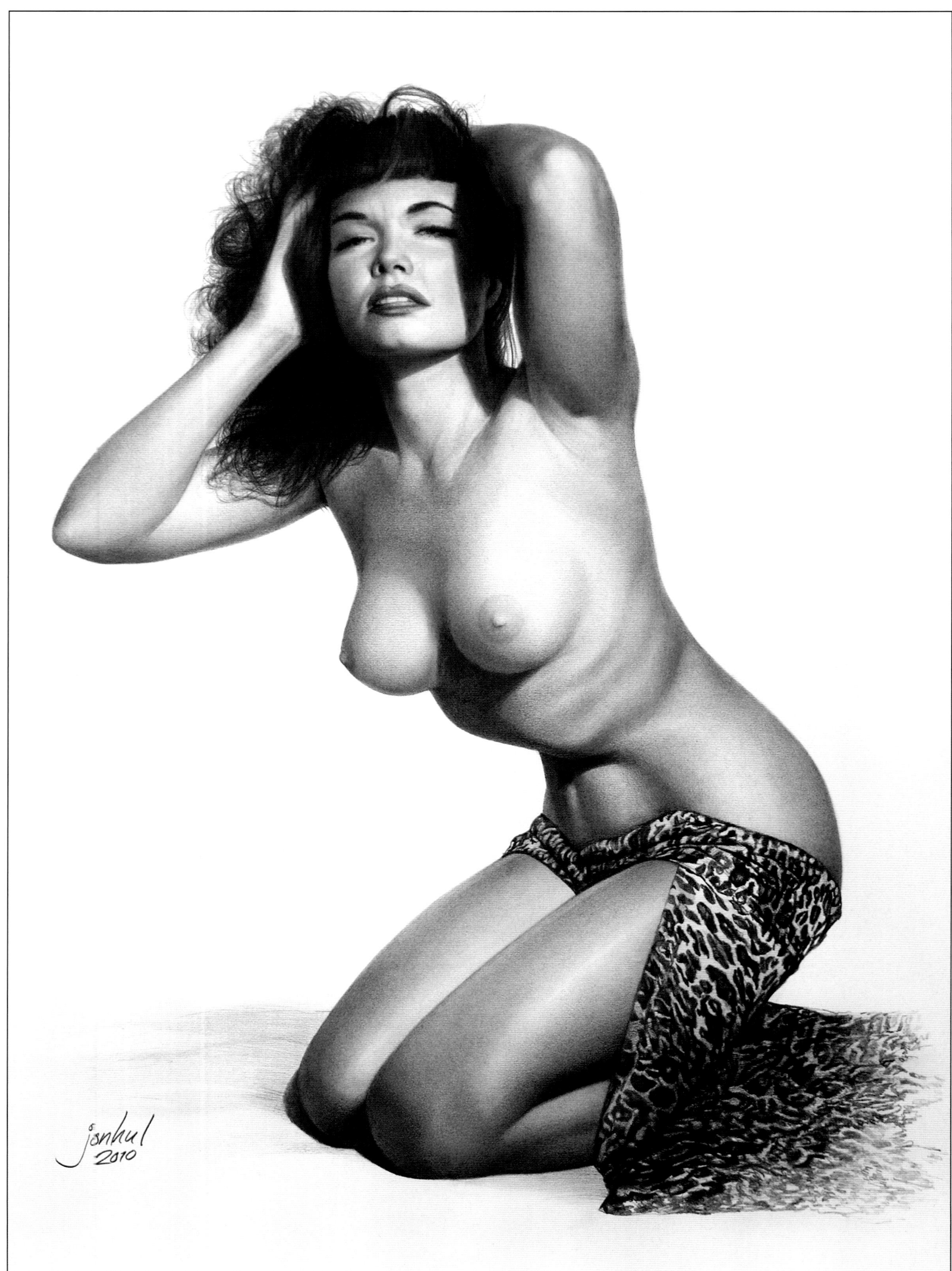

Forever Bettie

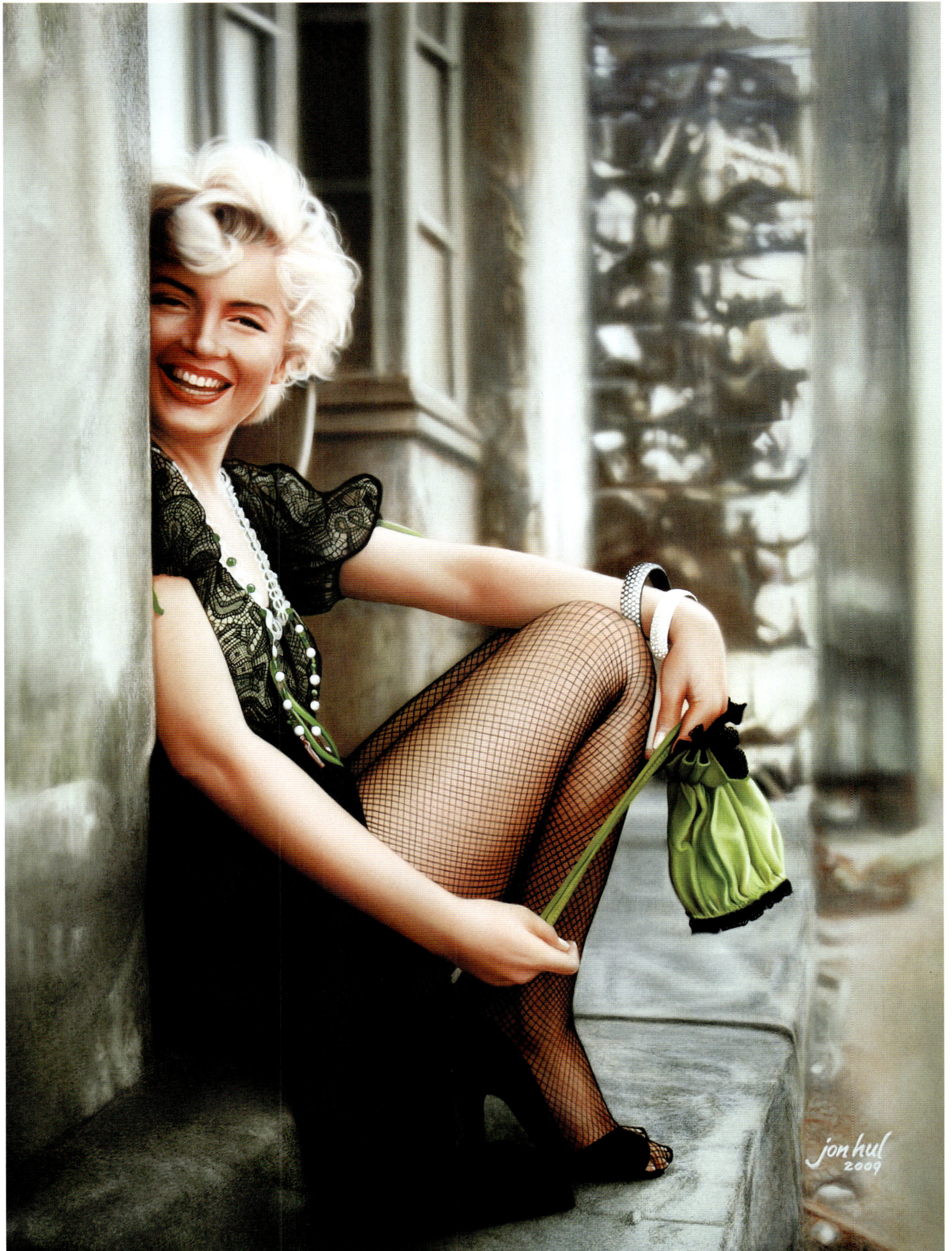

Sexy Marilyn

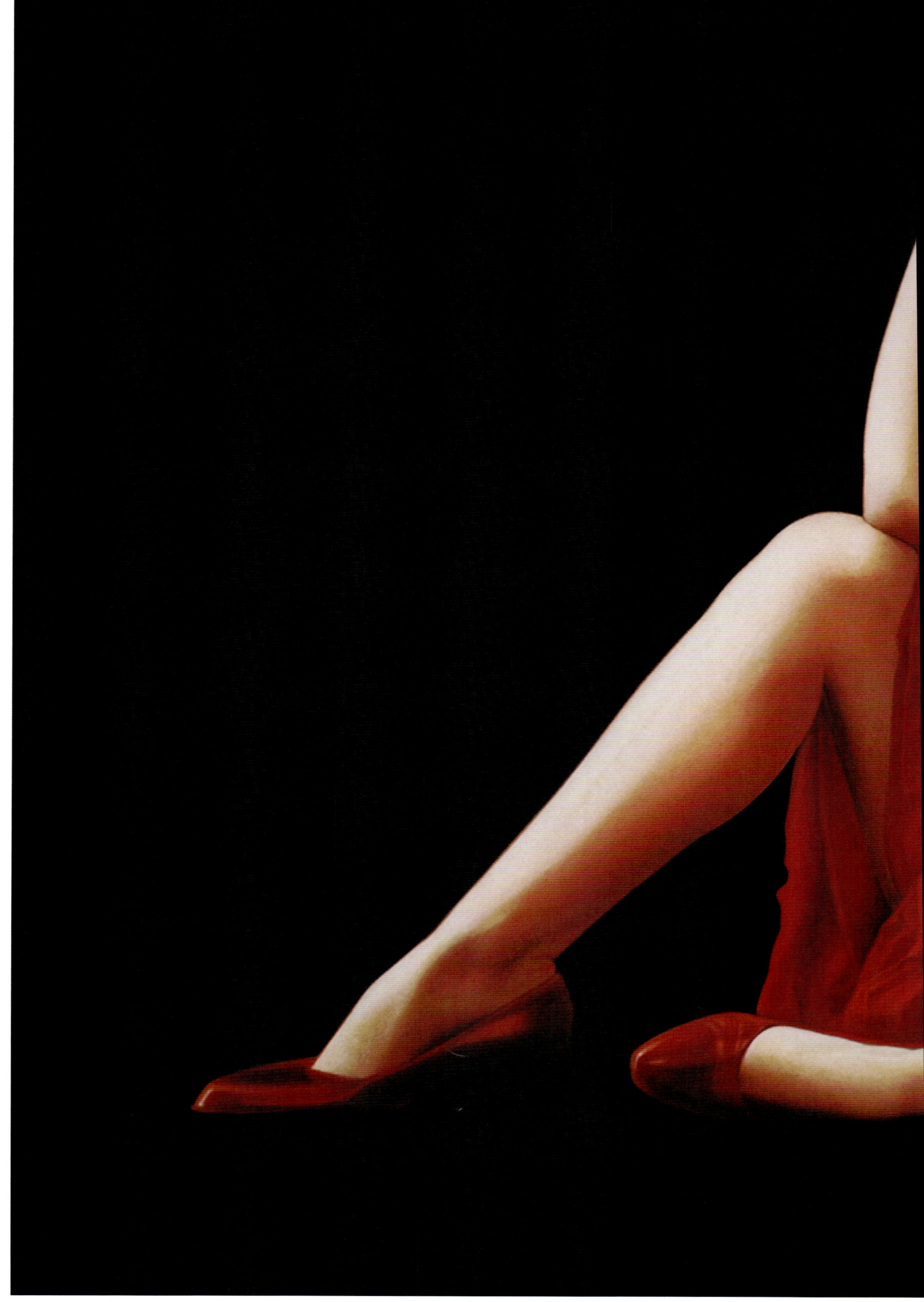

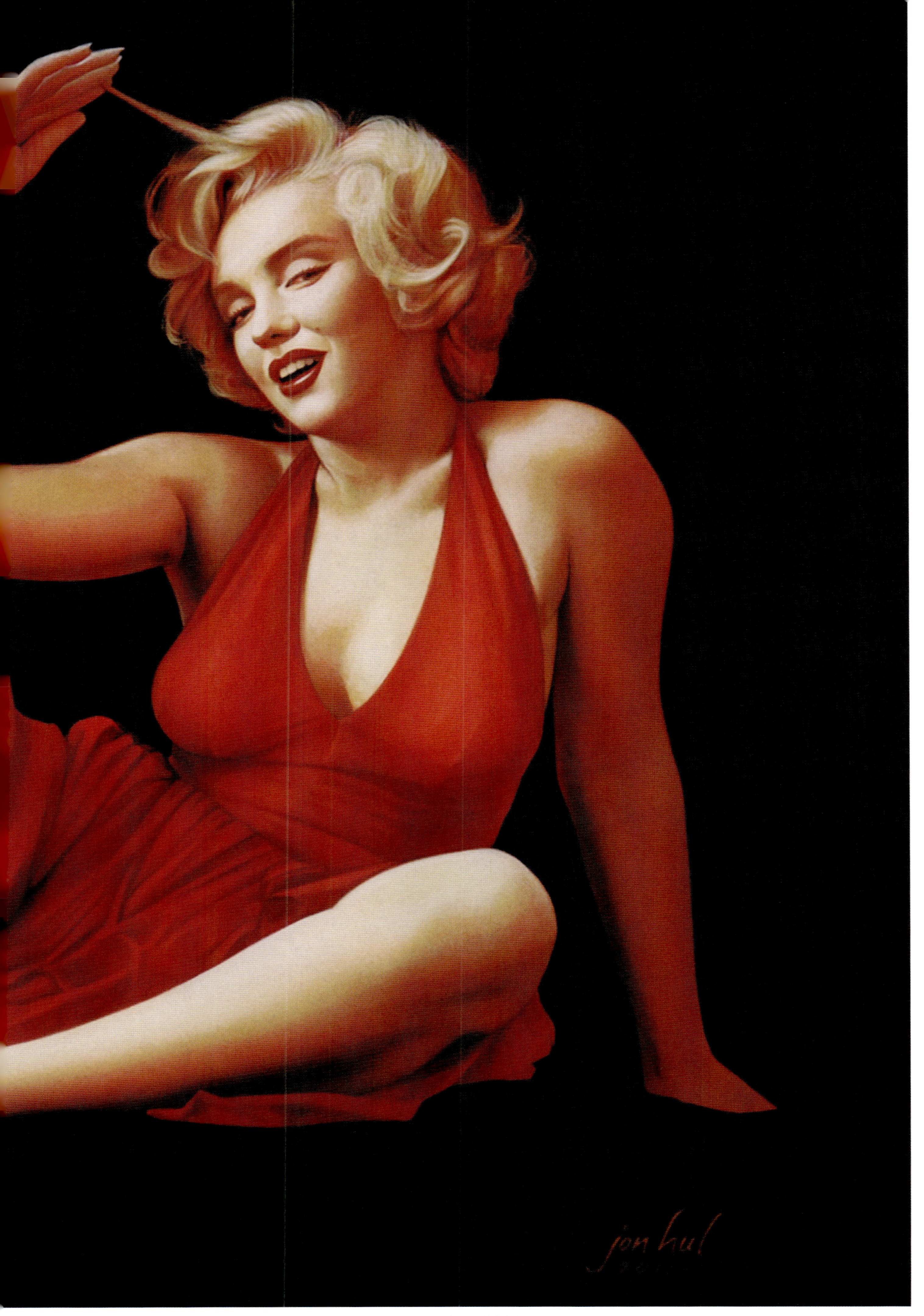

Unpredictable

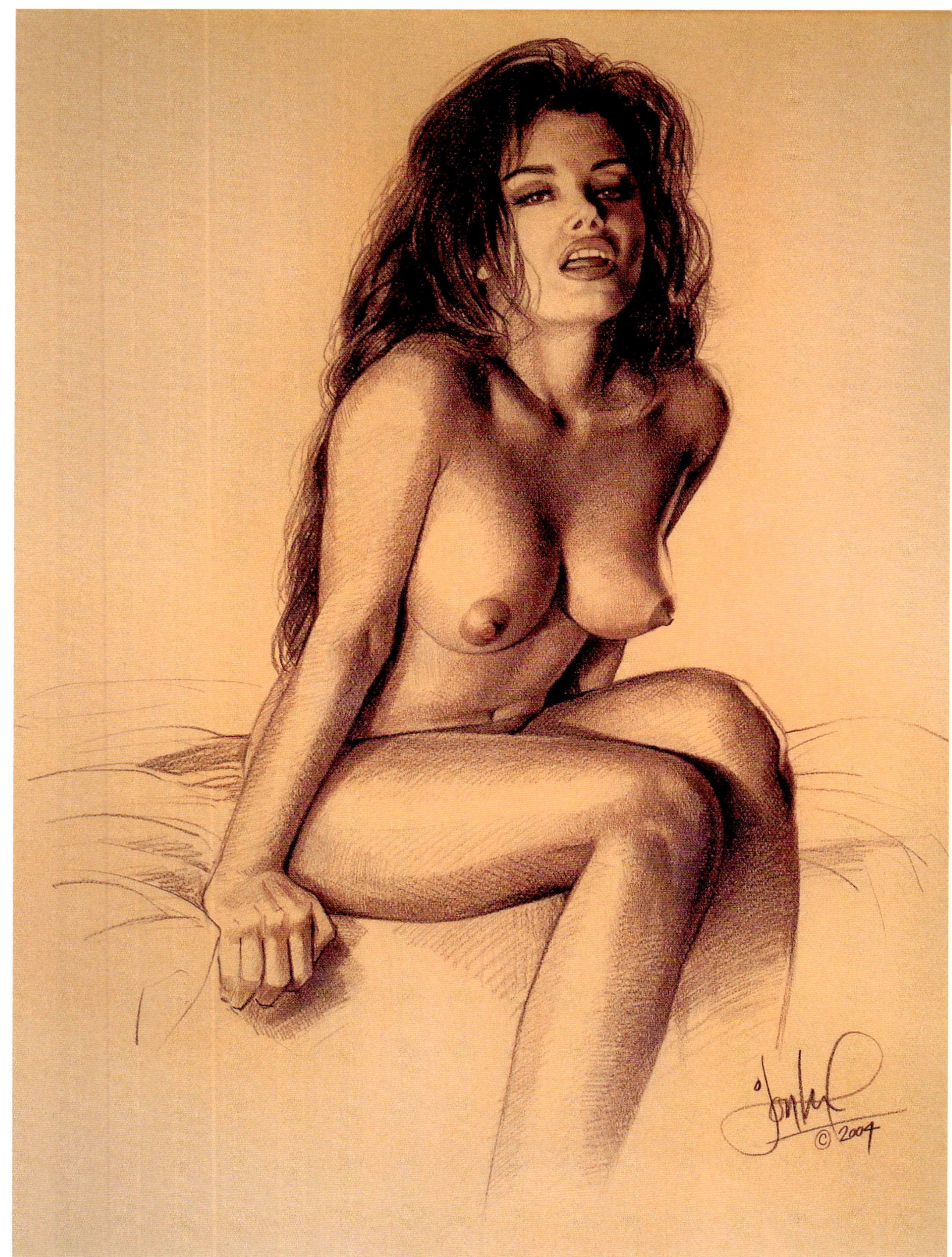

My Angel Baby - Study

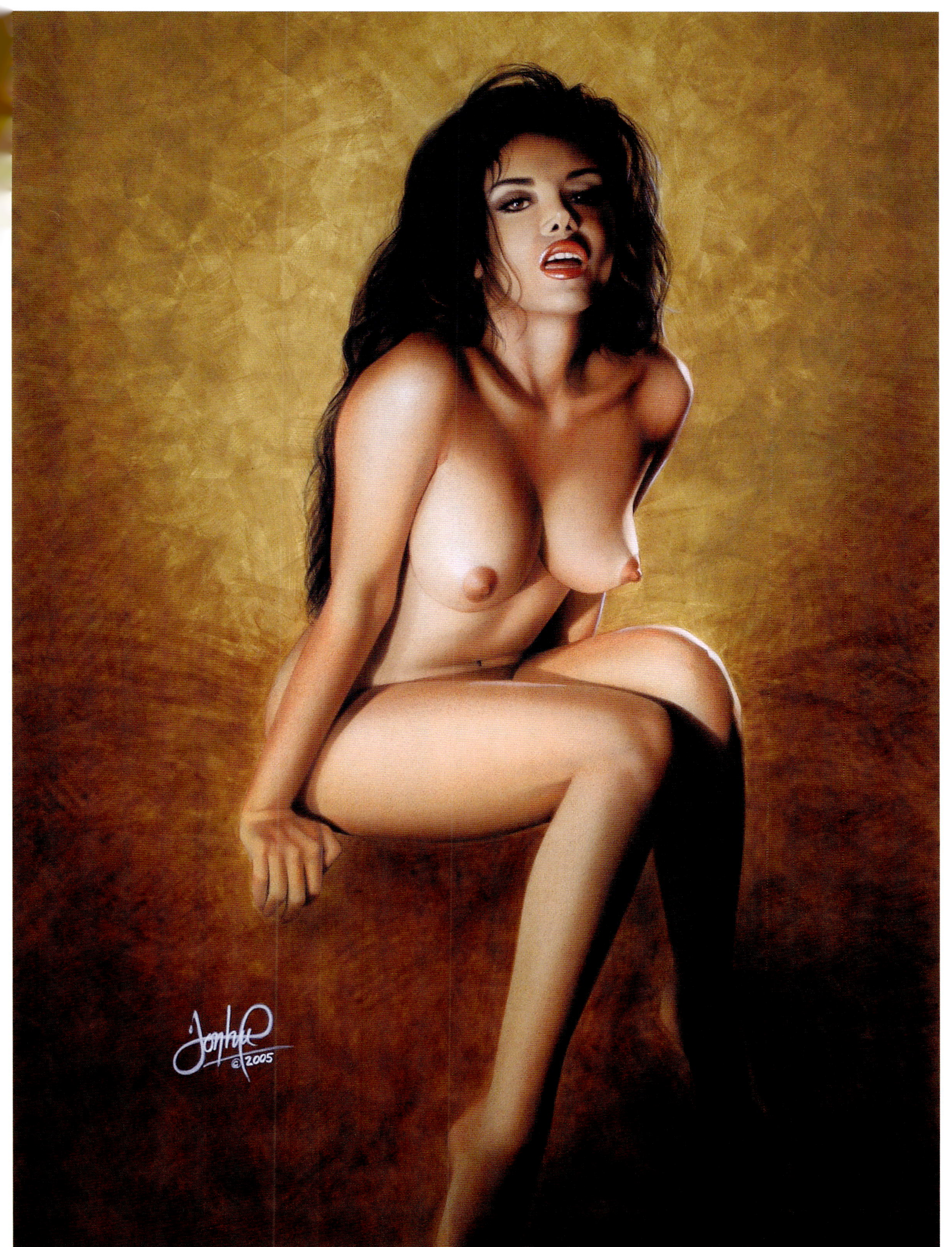

My Angel Baby

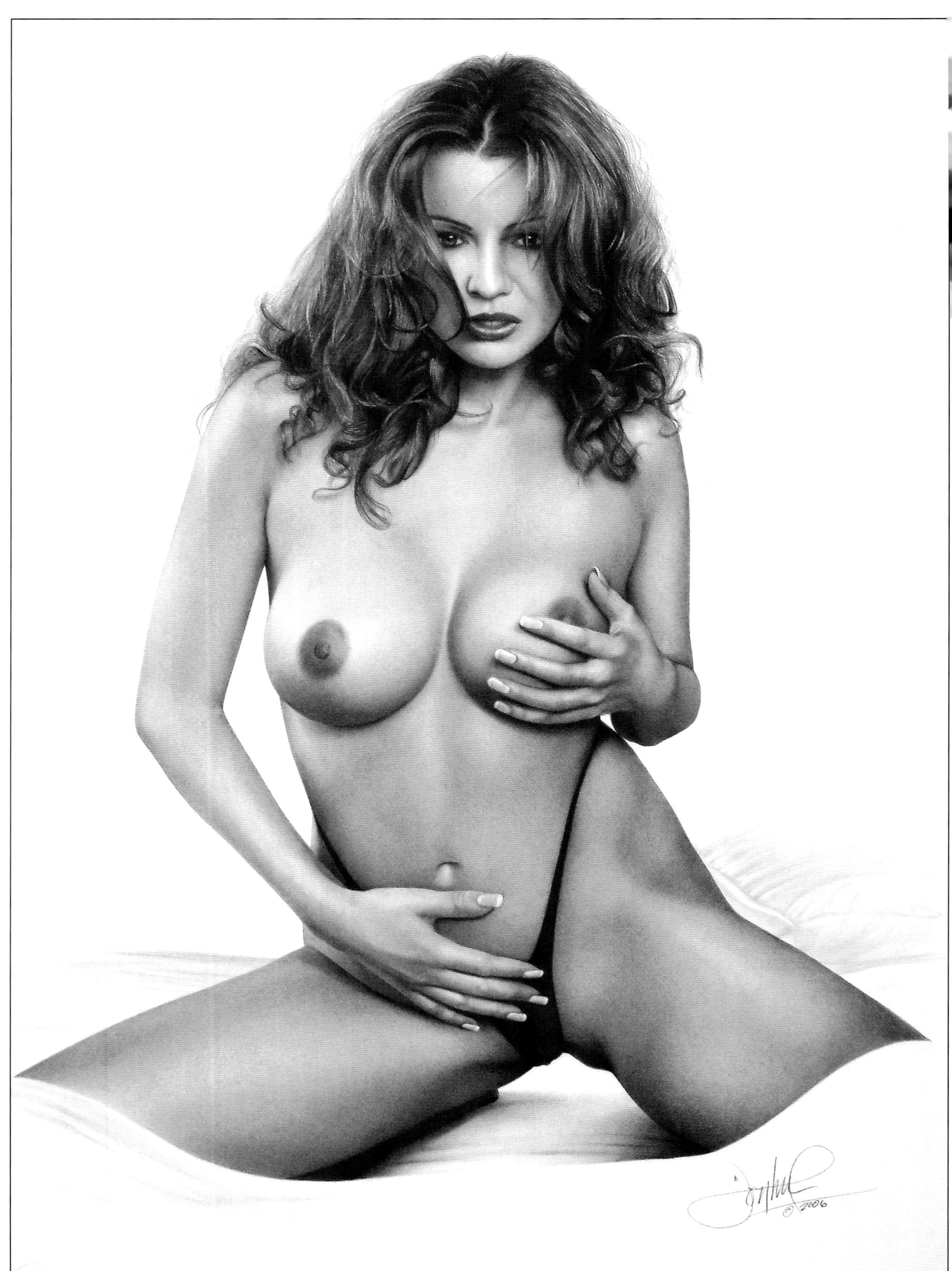

Afternoon Delight

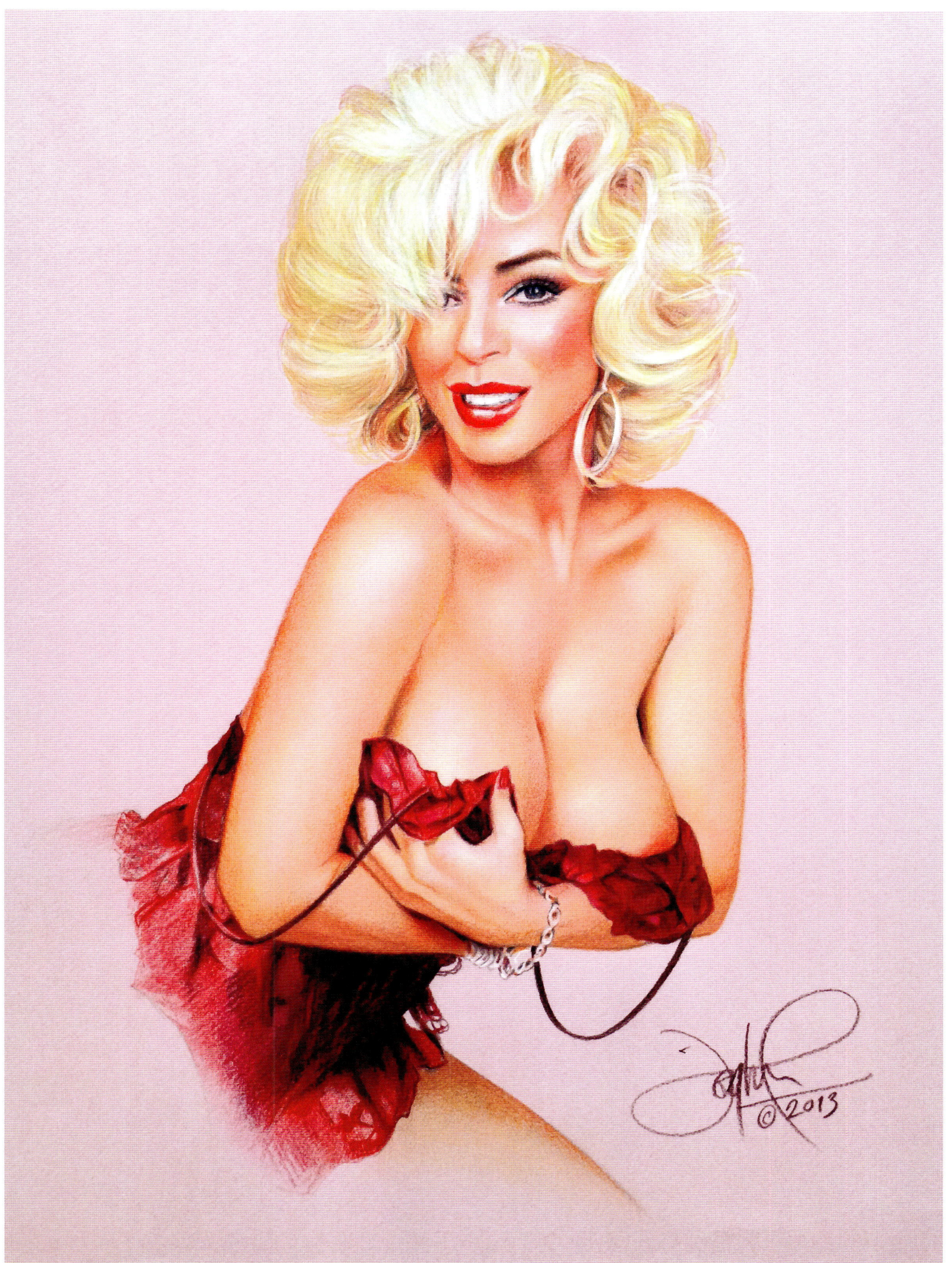

Luv Bundle

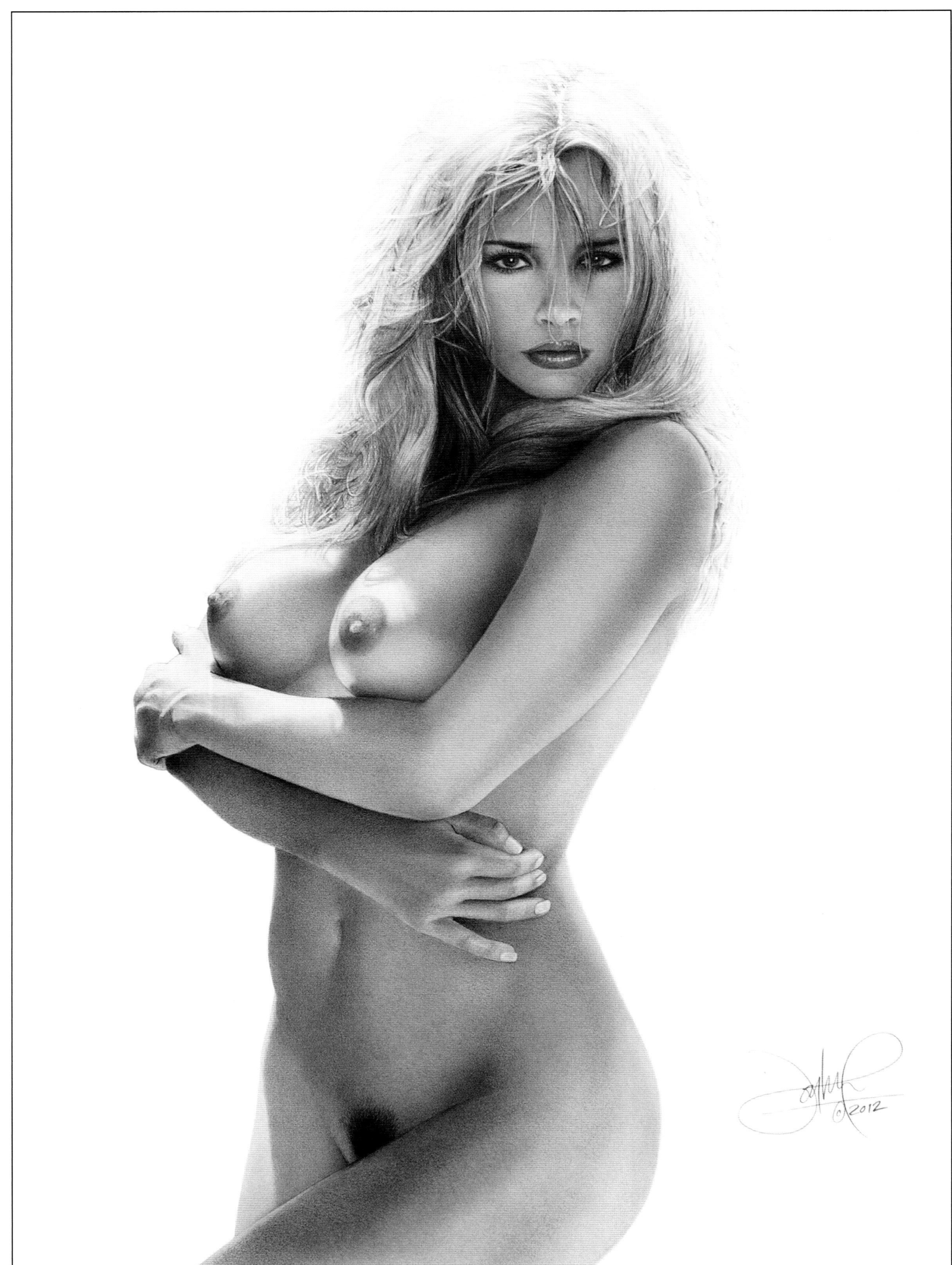

Cradle Baby

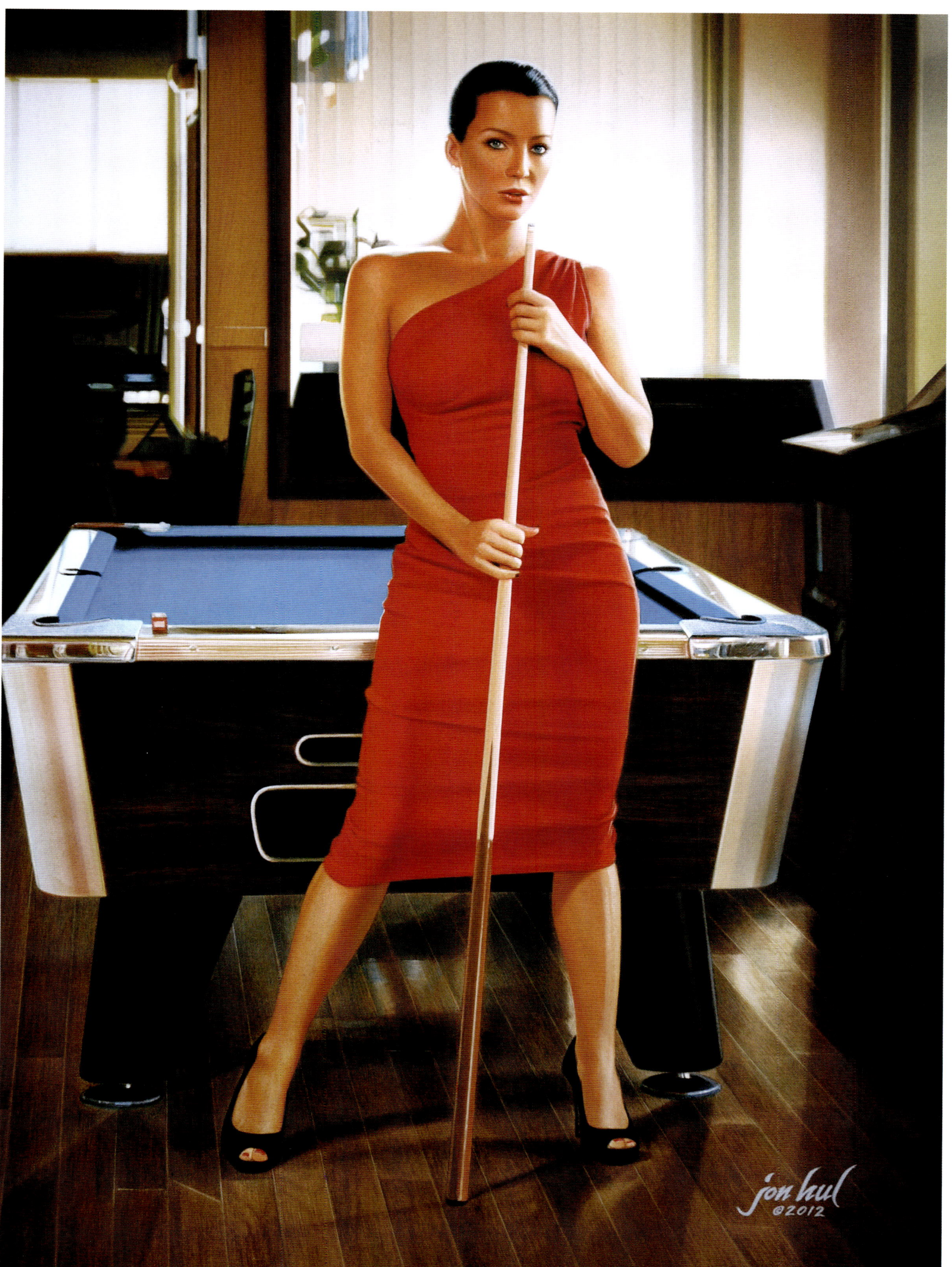

Red Hot Hustler

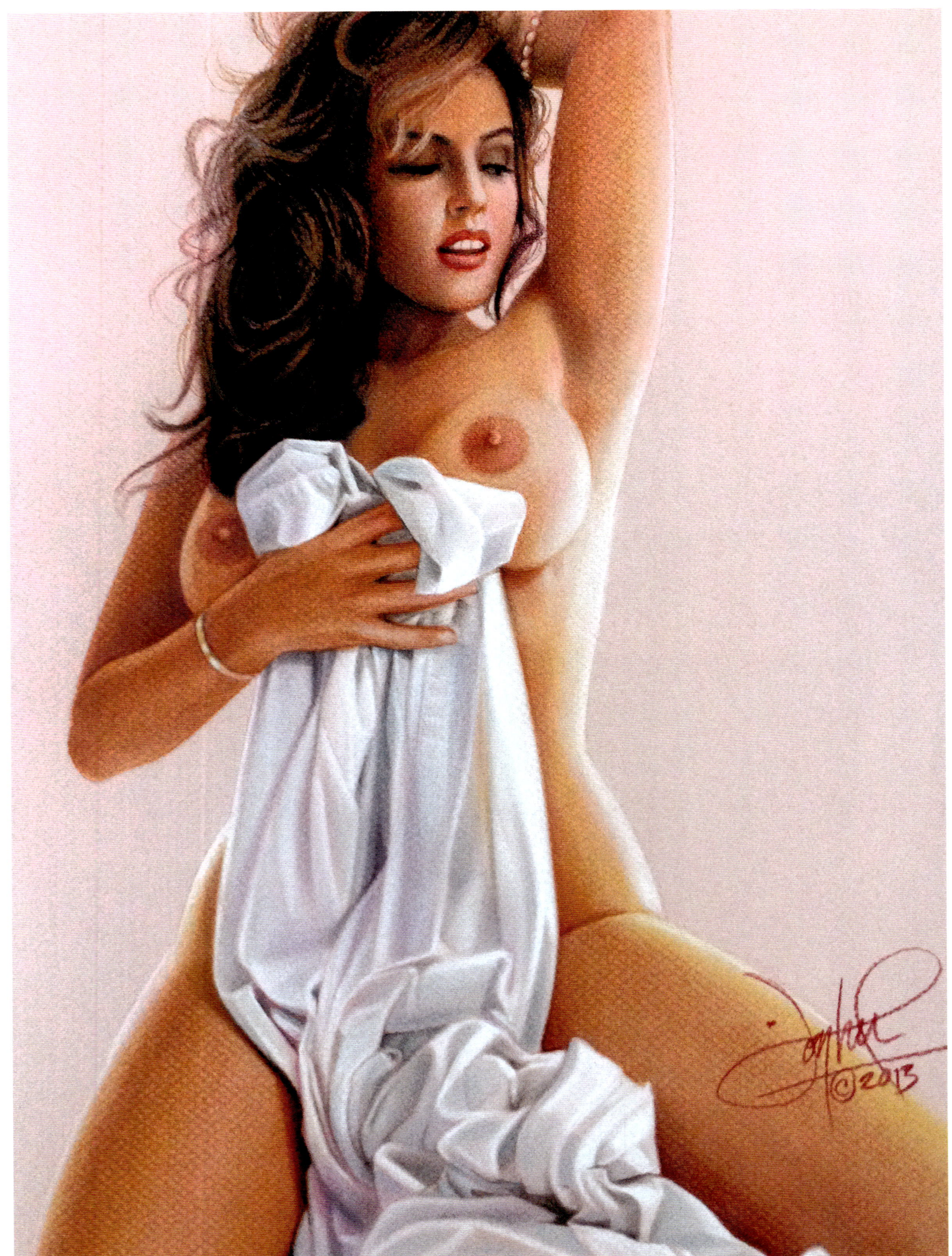

More Need Indeed

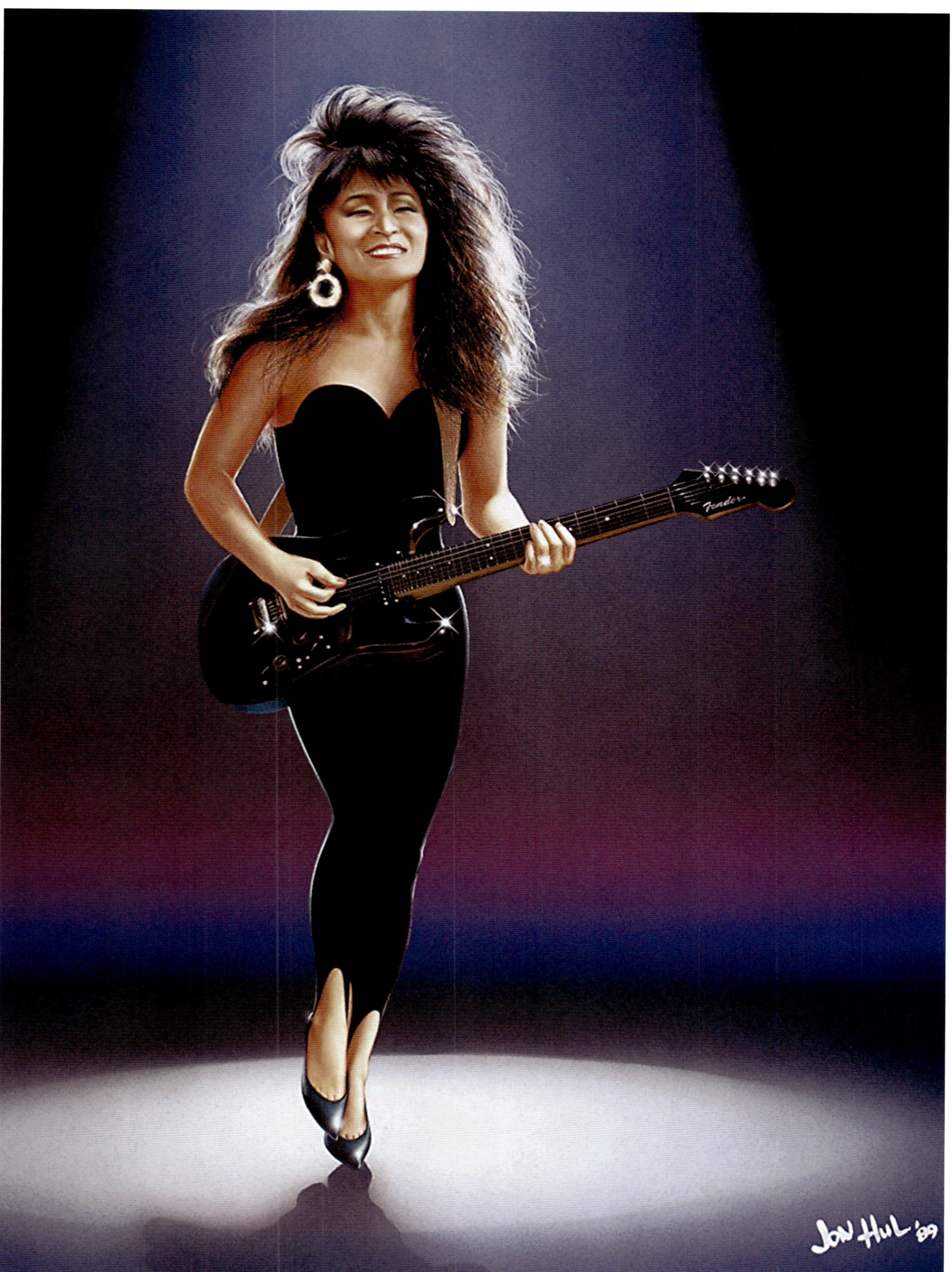

Prance of the Performer

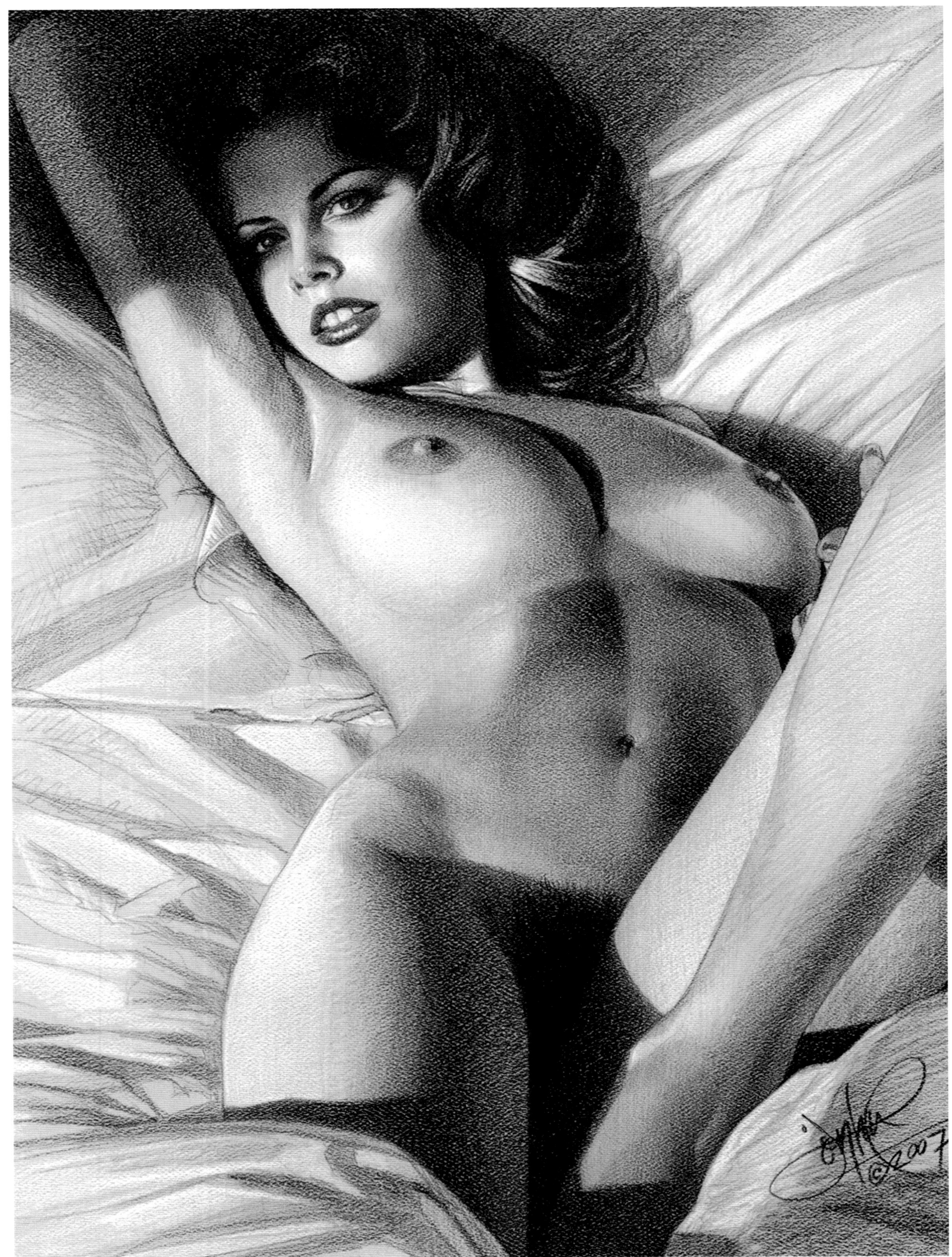

The Craving - Pencil Study

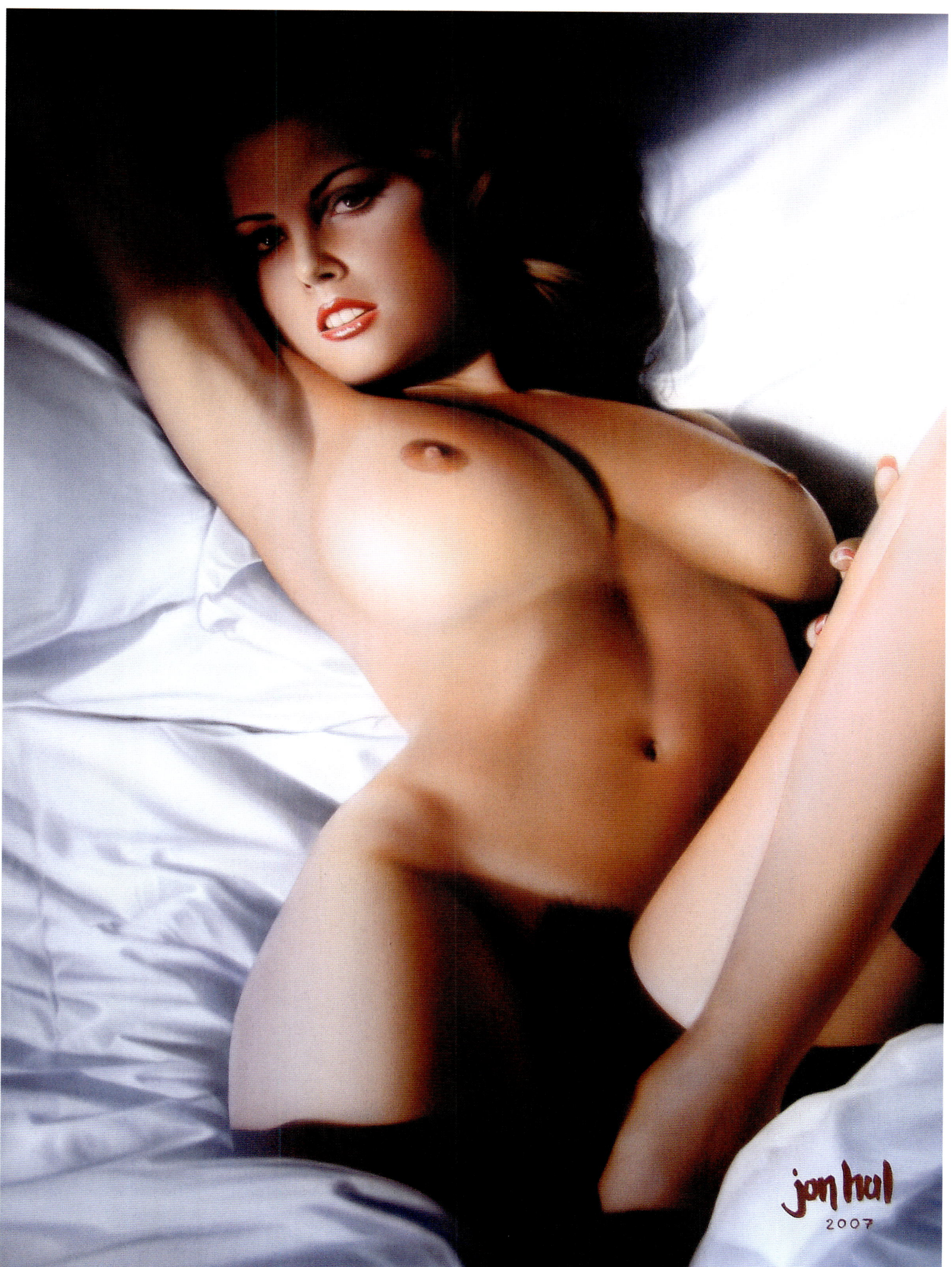

The Craving

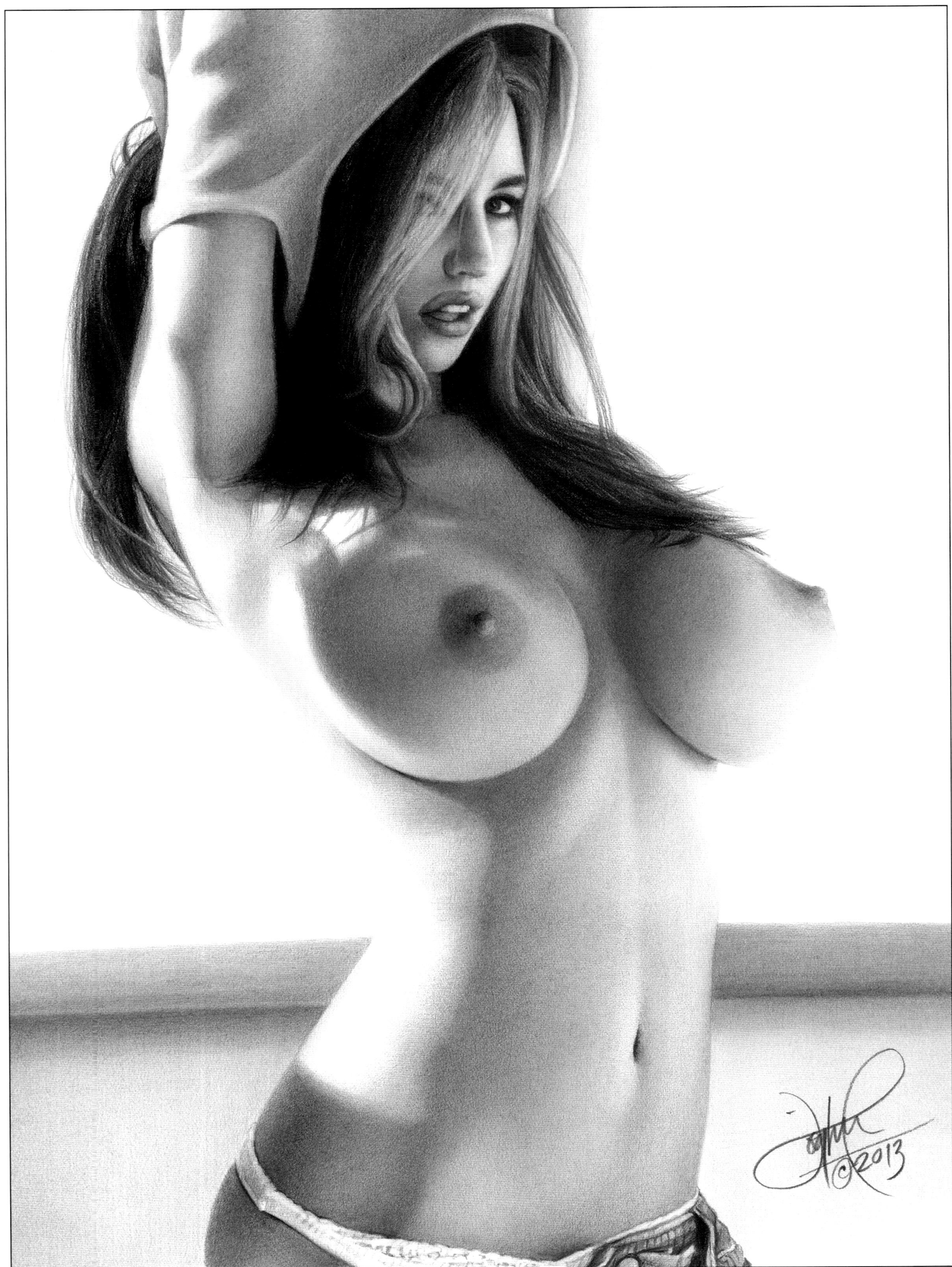

The Flip Side

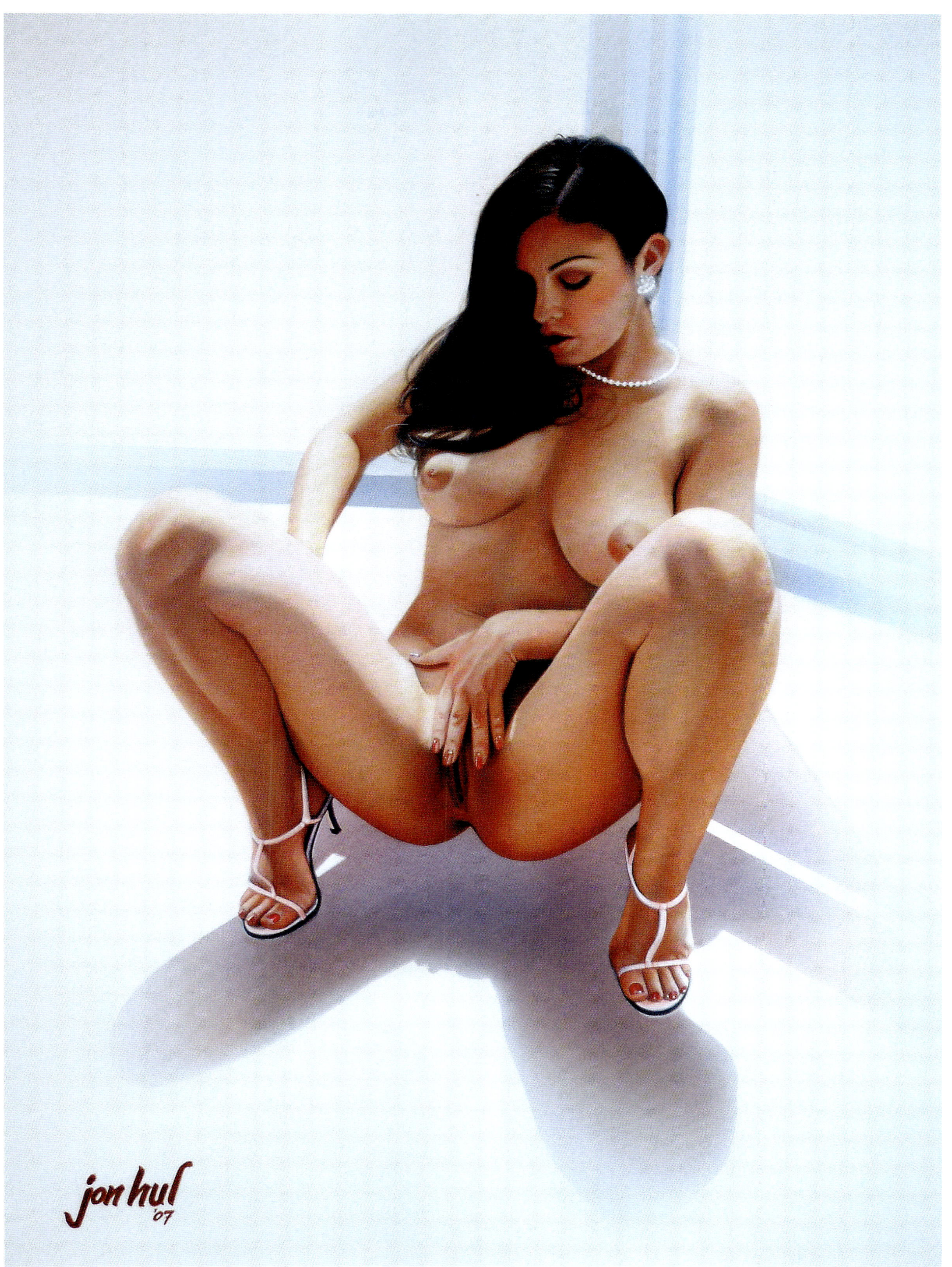

Pre-Occupied

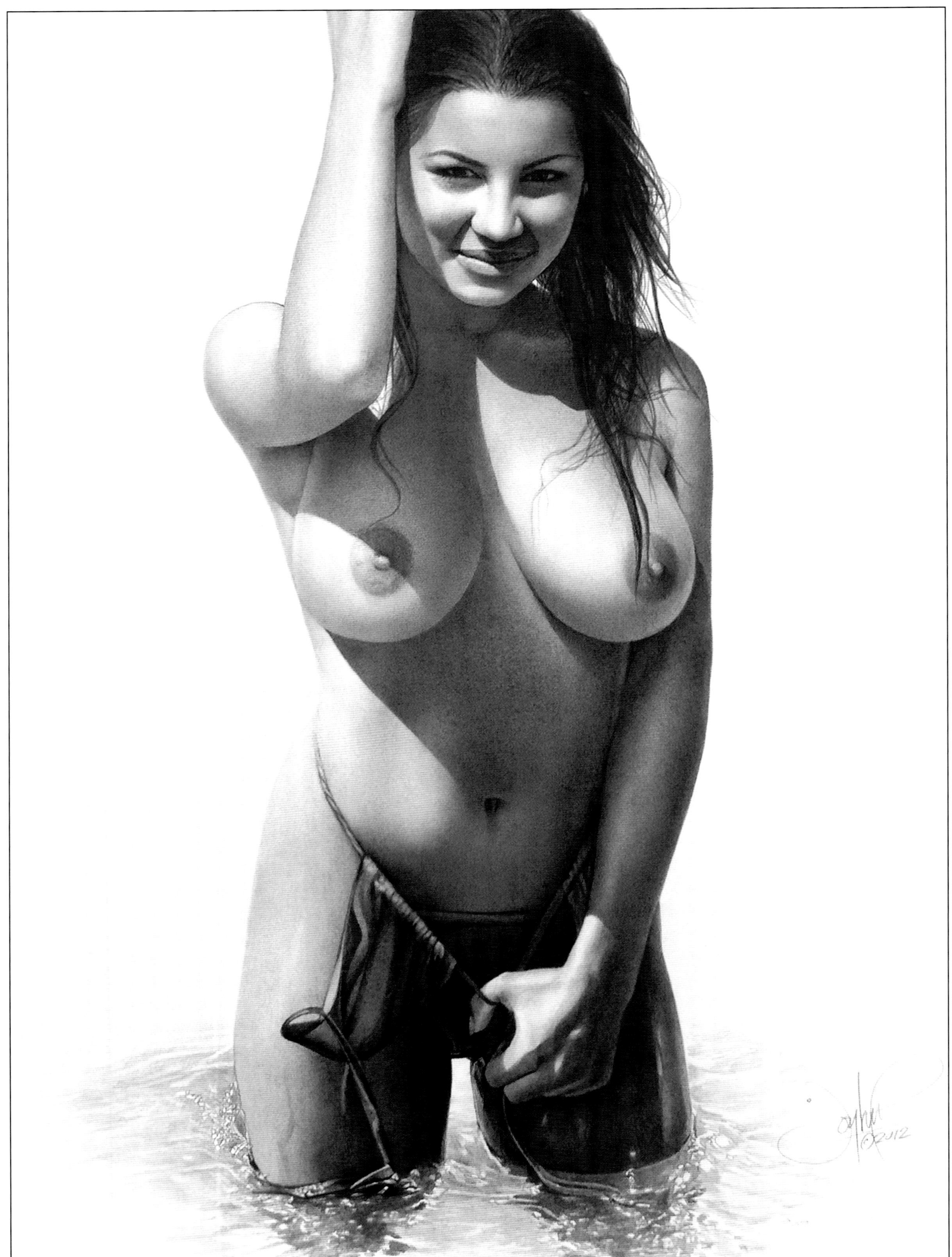

Girl In Water

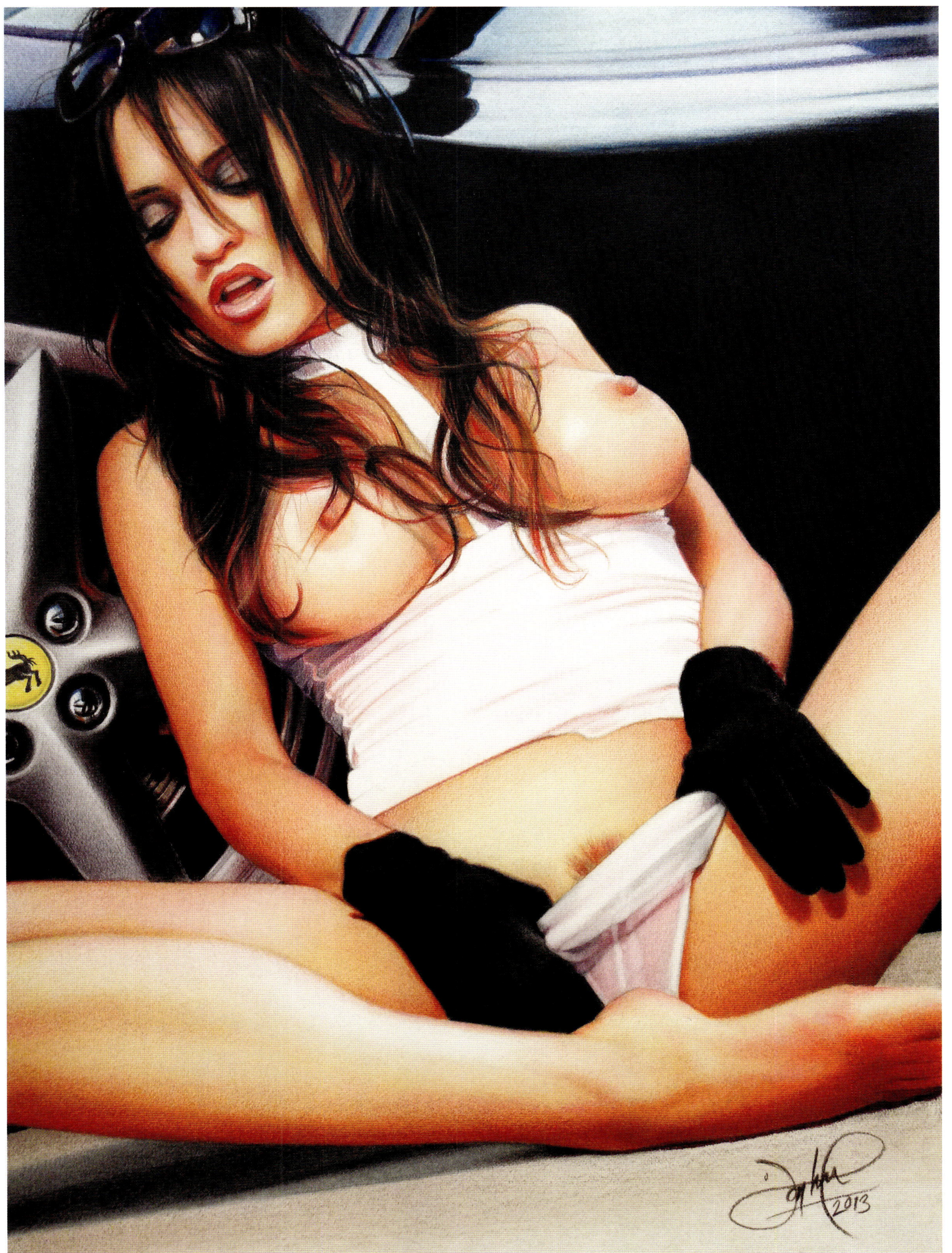

Drive It Like You Stole It

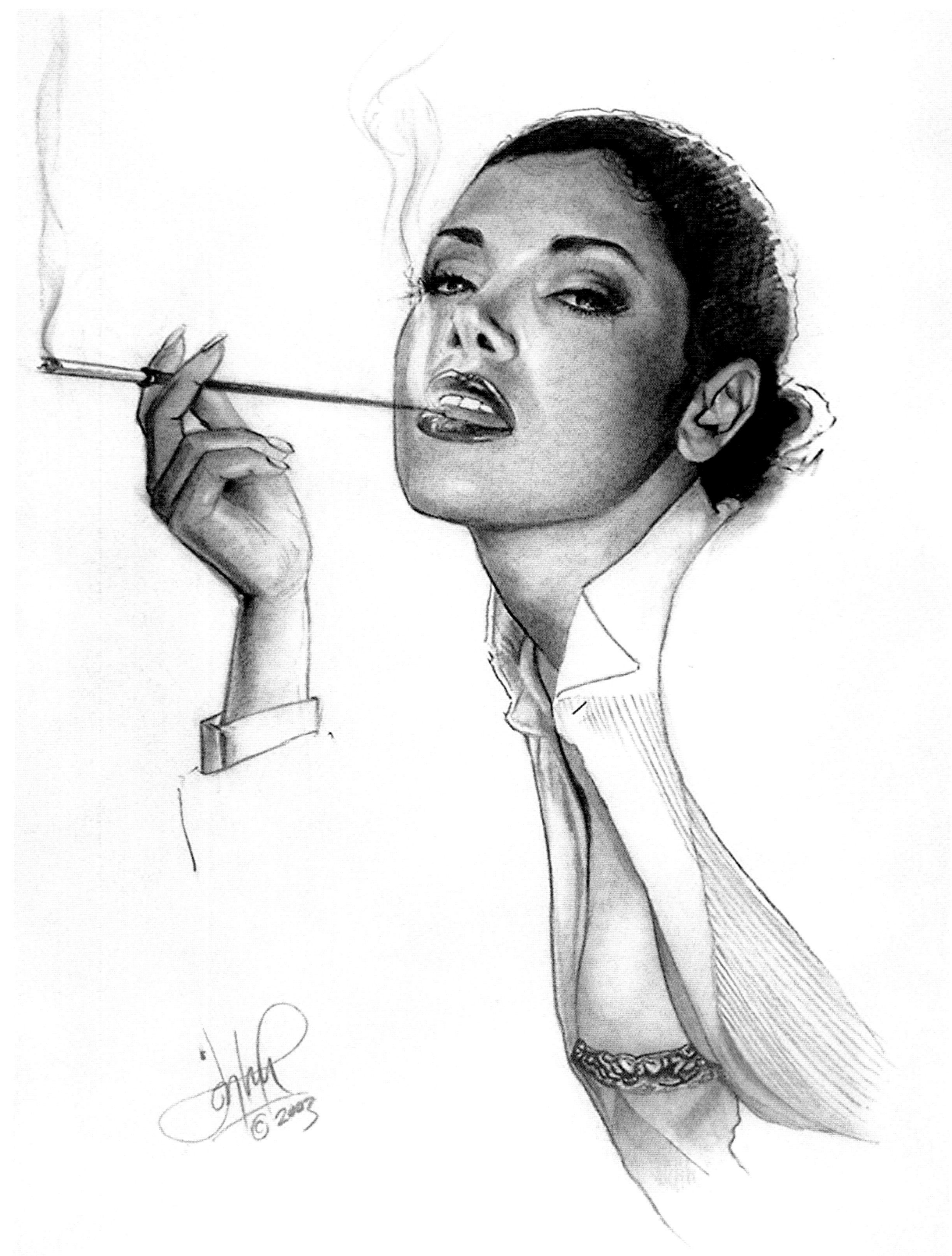

Smokin' - Pencil Study

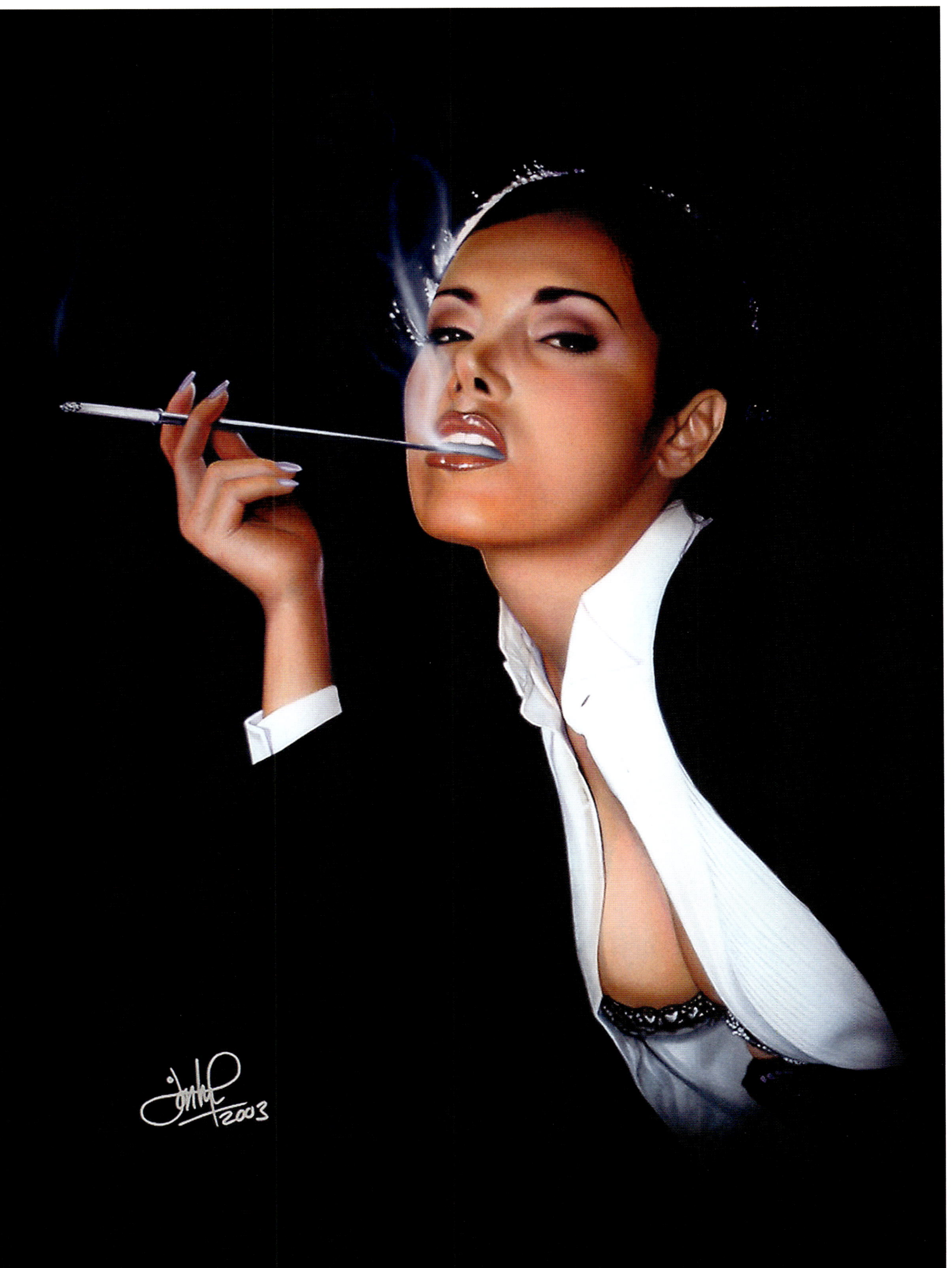

Smokin'

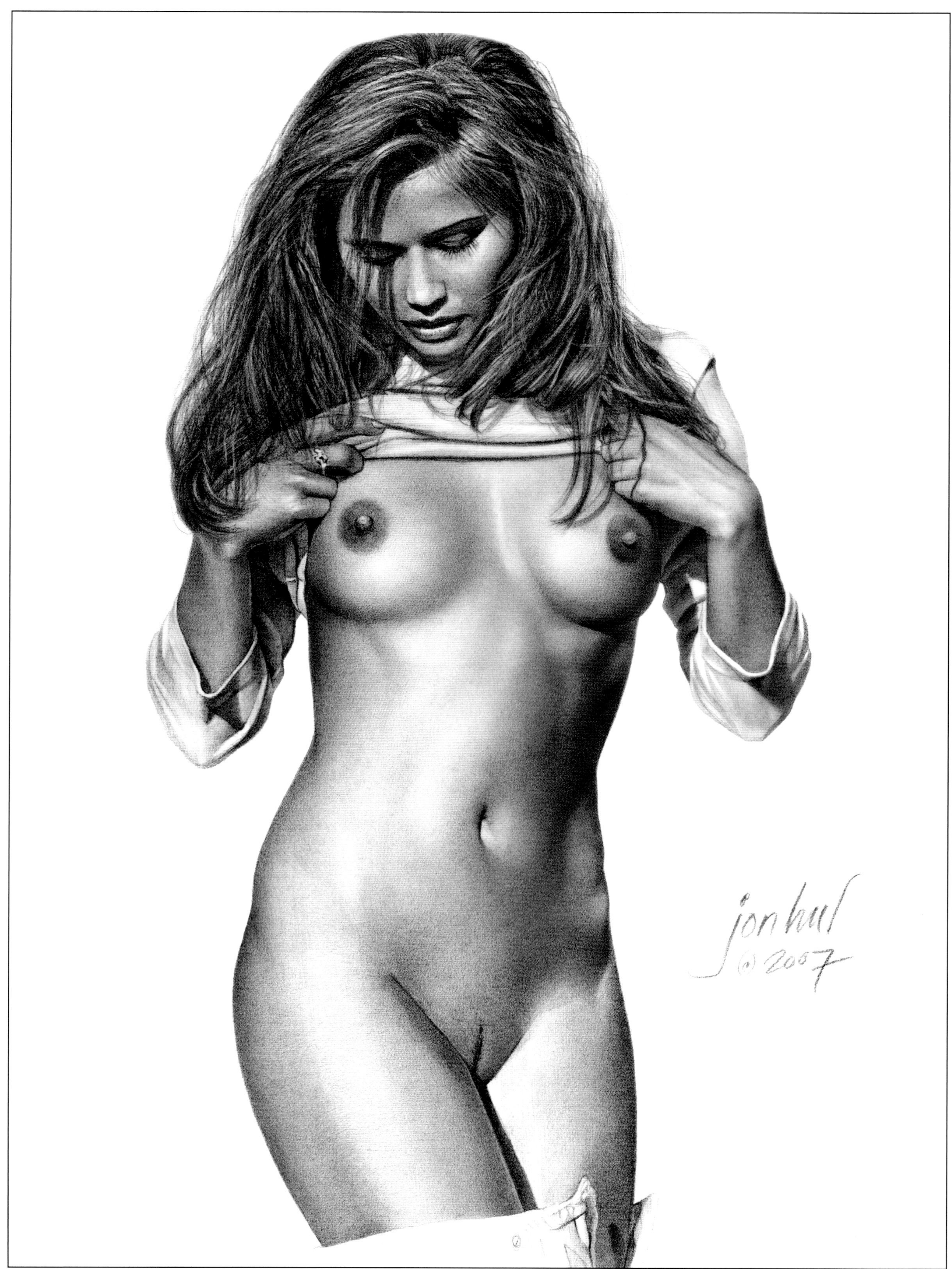

Subtle Dreams

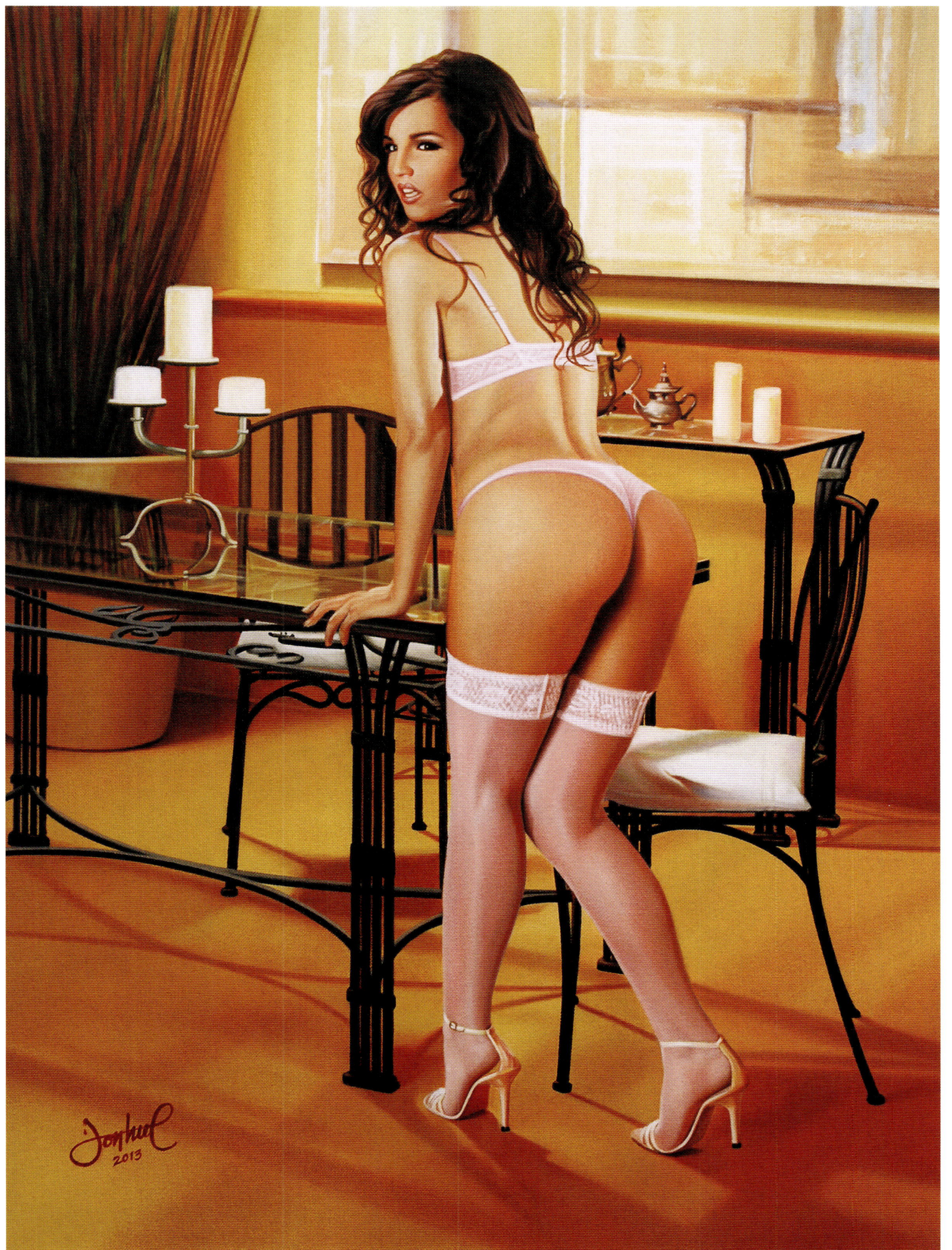

Perfect Time

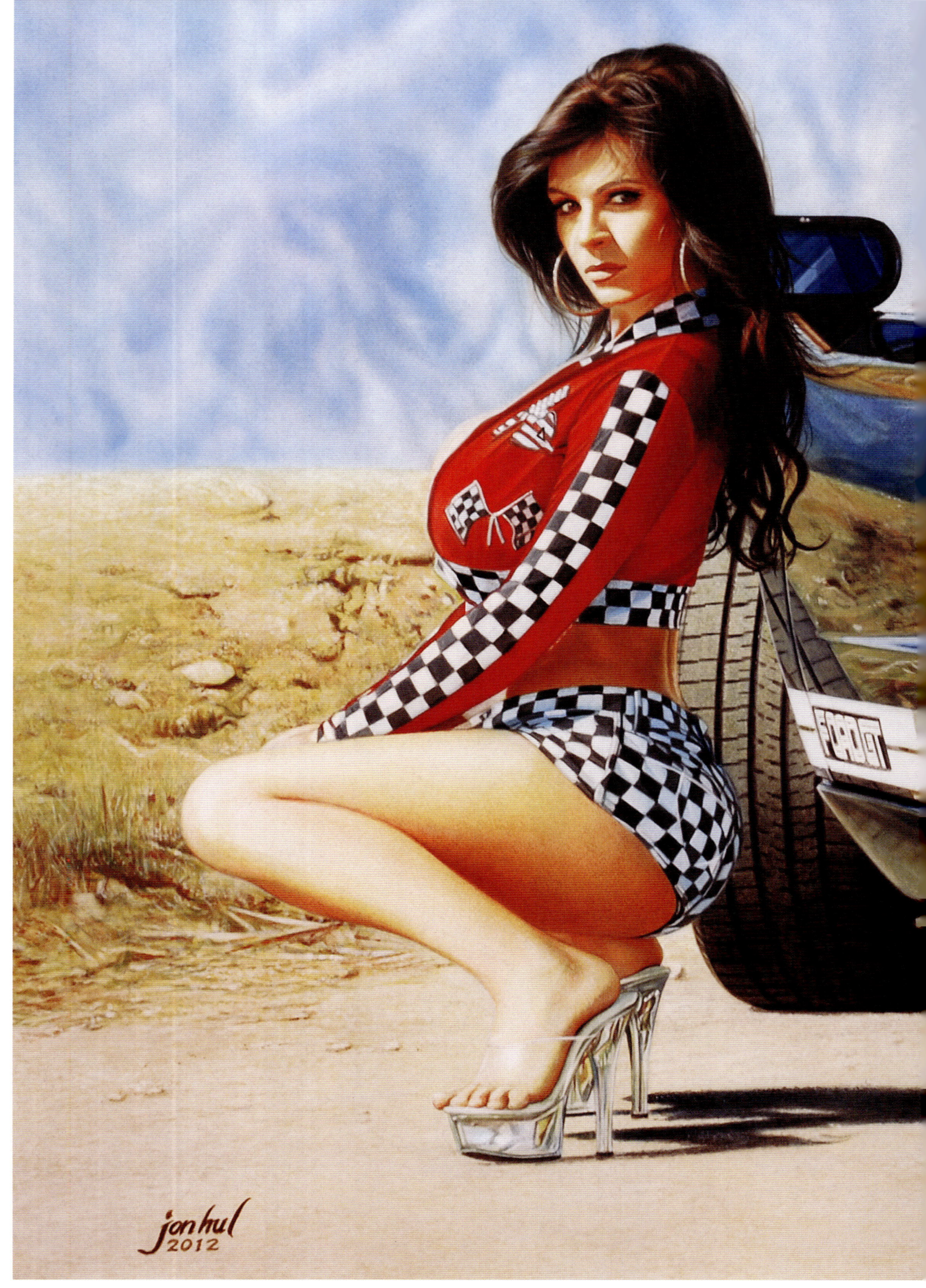
jonhul
2012

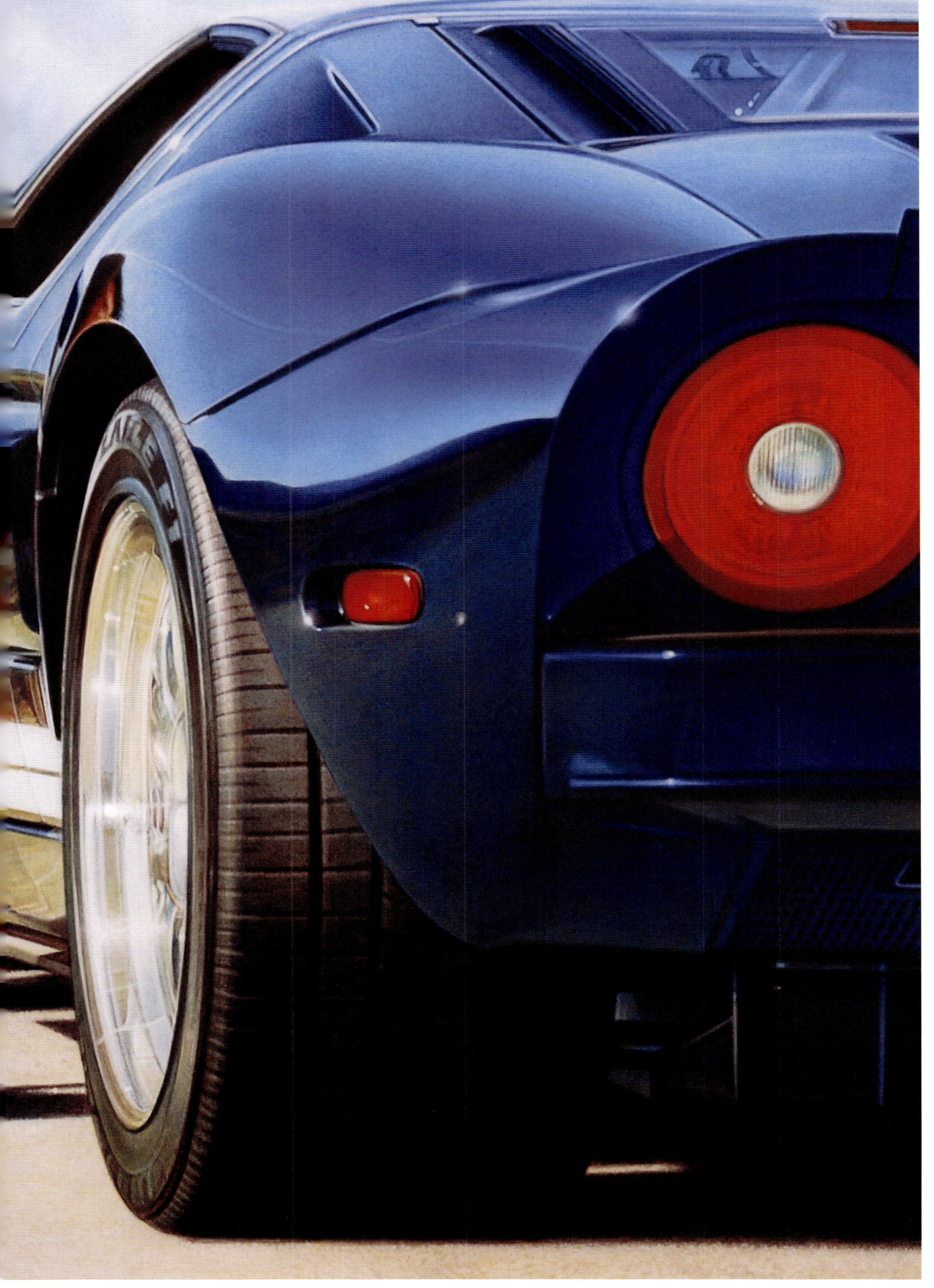

Revved Up

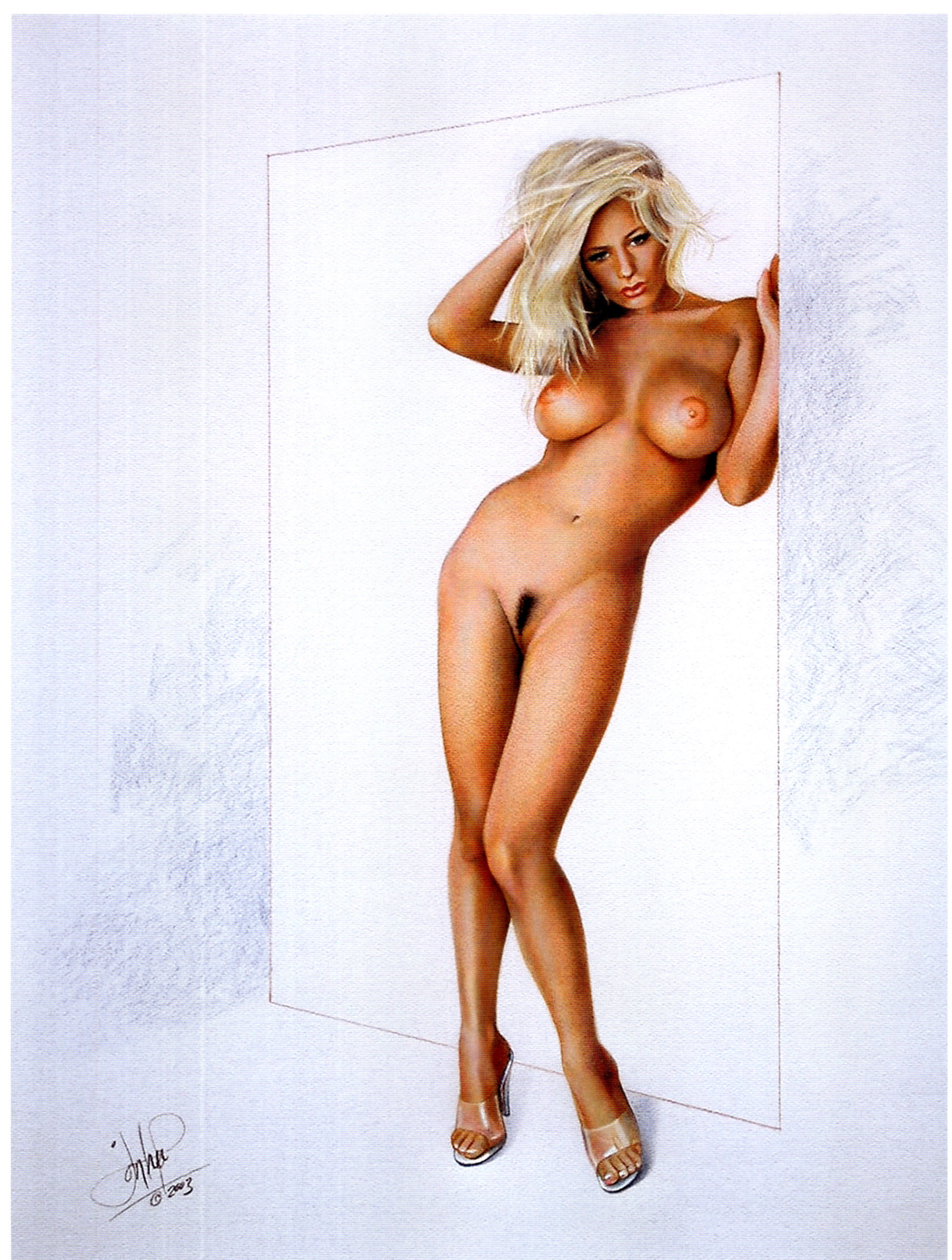

Inward Looking Outside

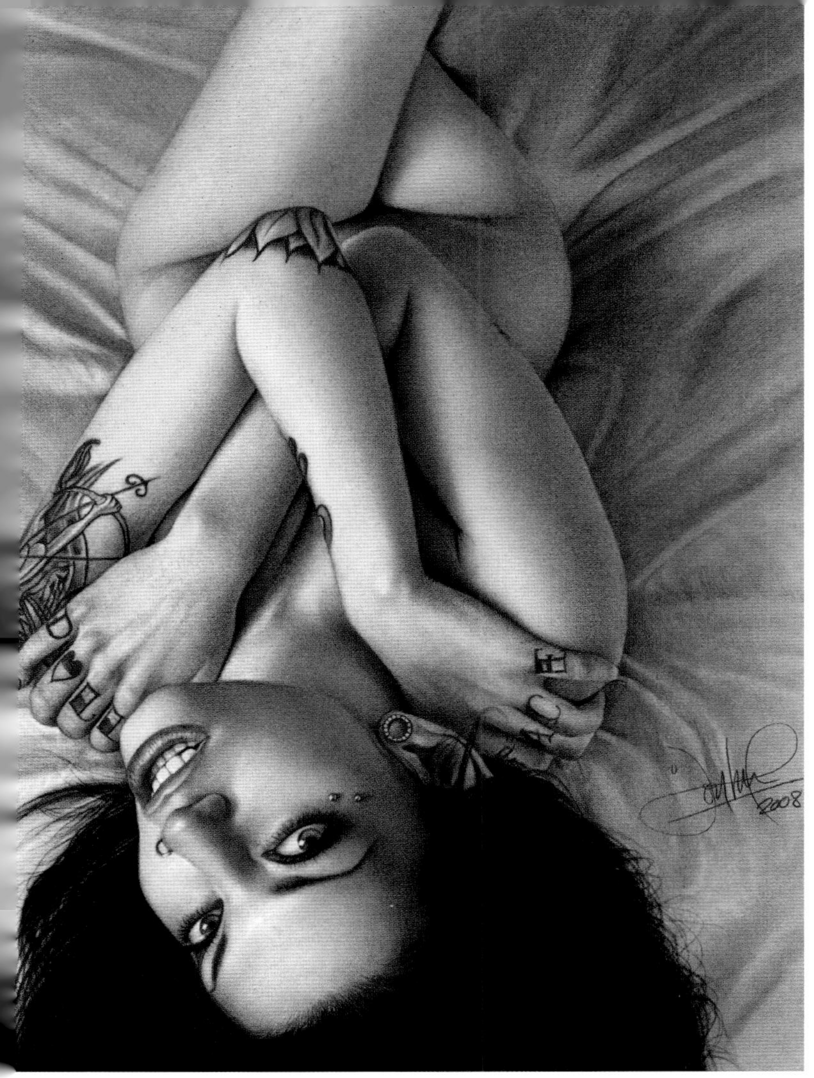

Doll Face

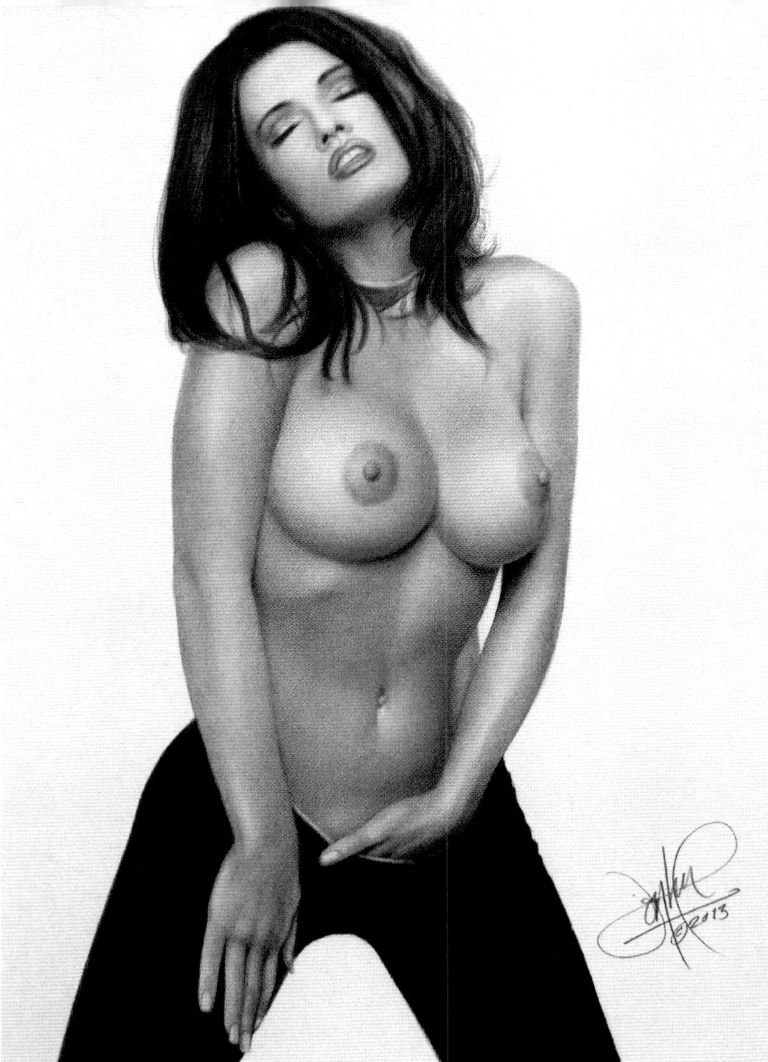

Midas Touch

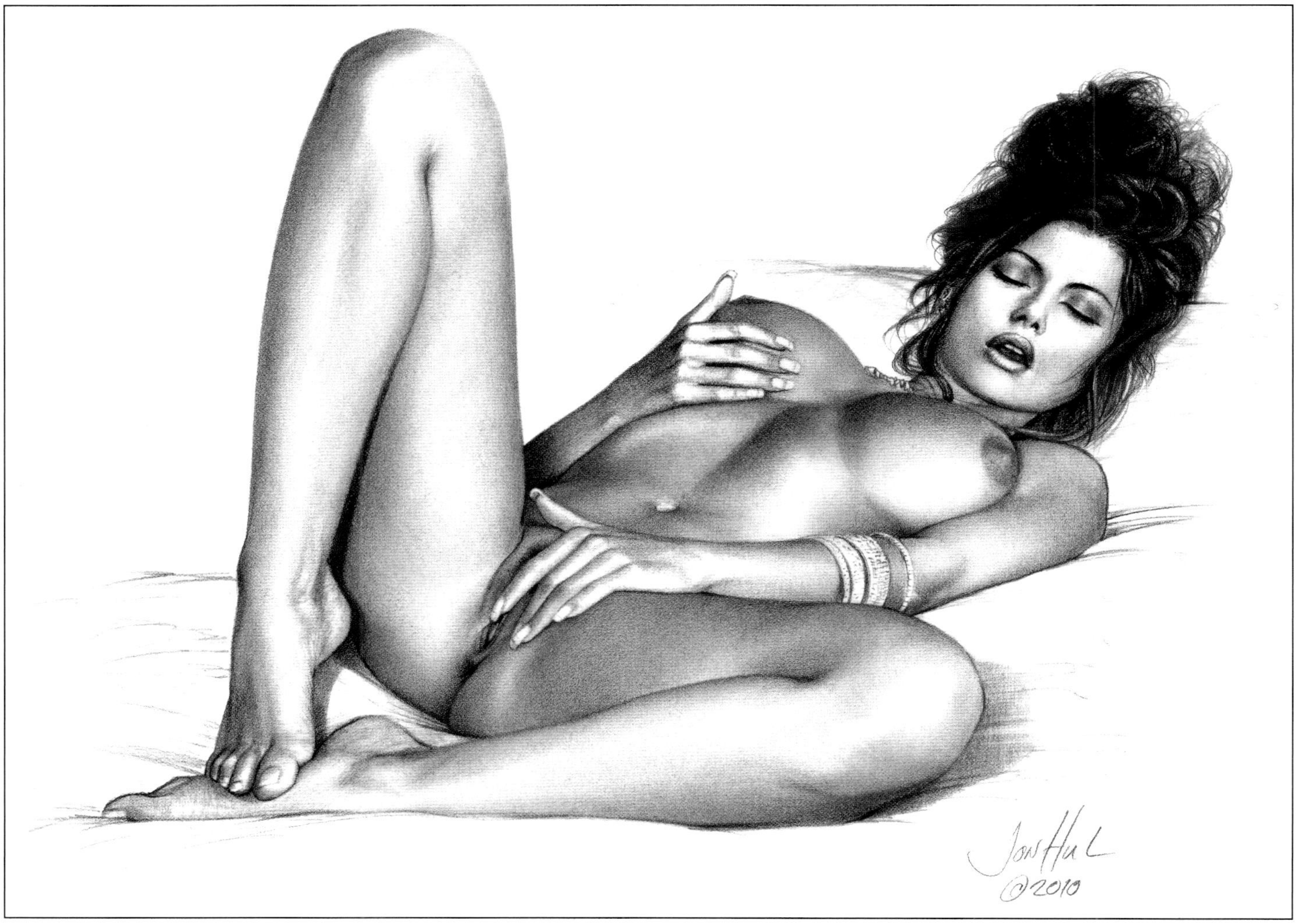

Hot Dipping Cream

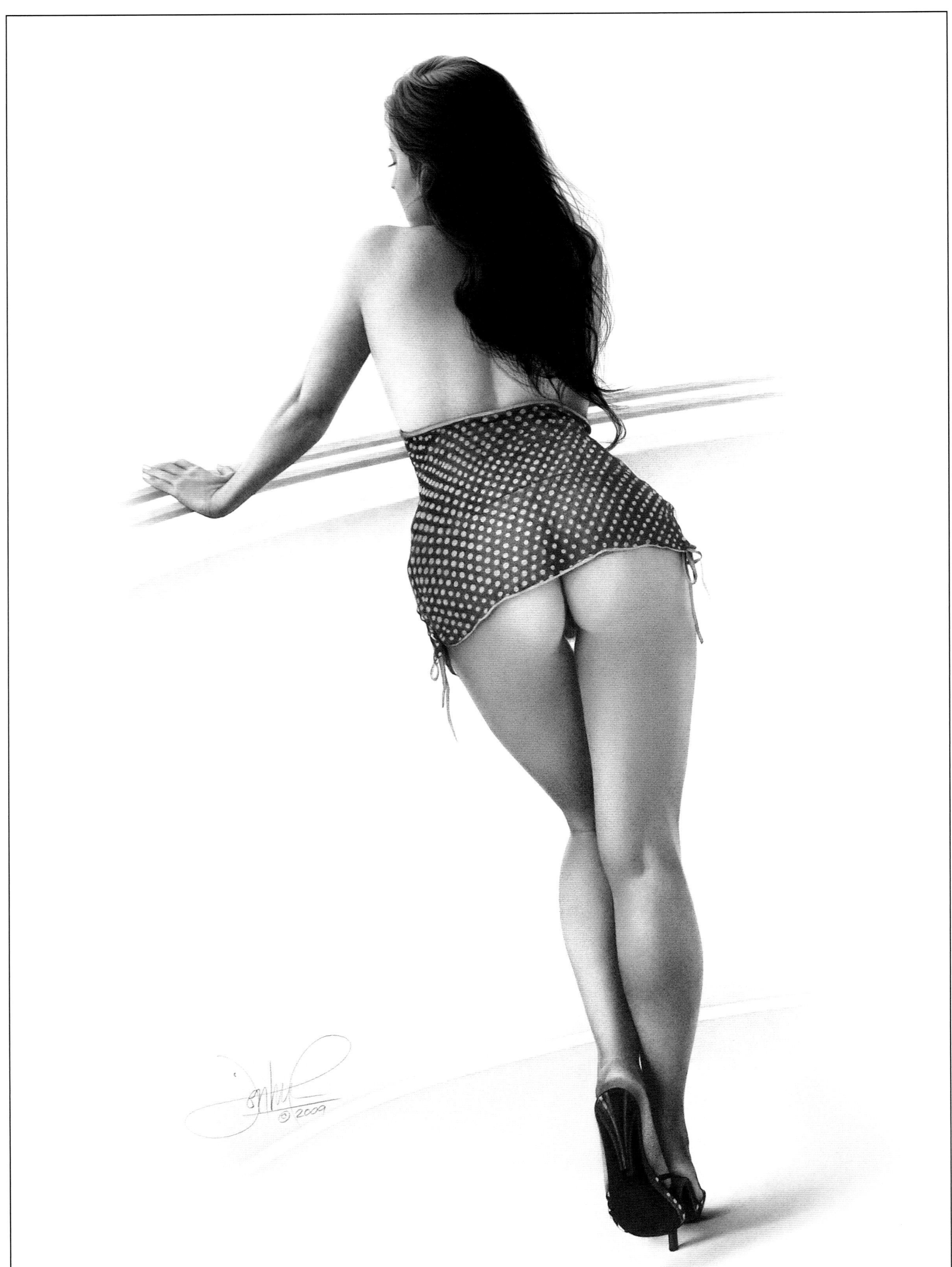

Perfect View - Pencil Study

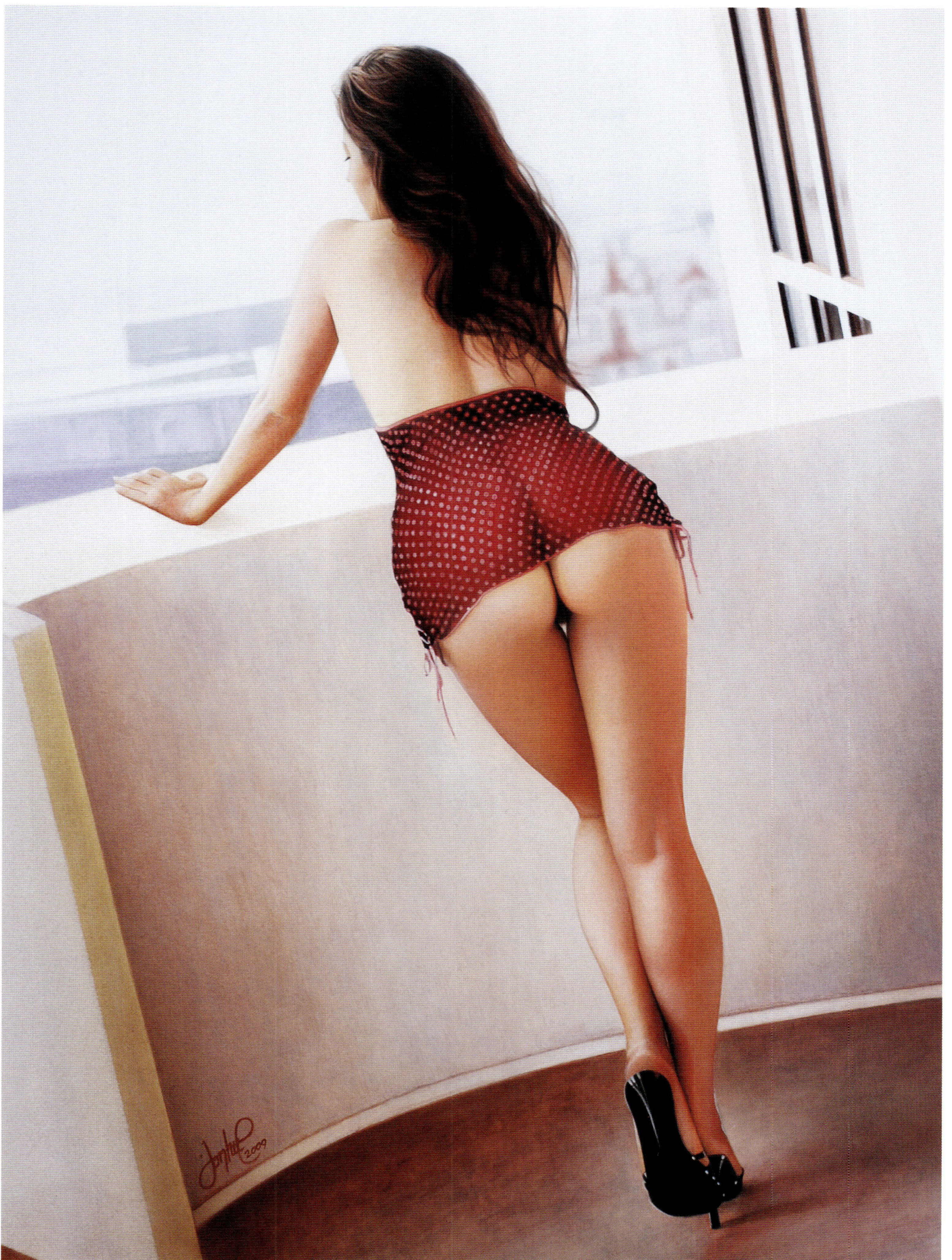

Perfect View

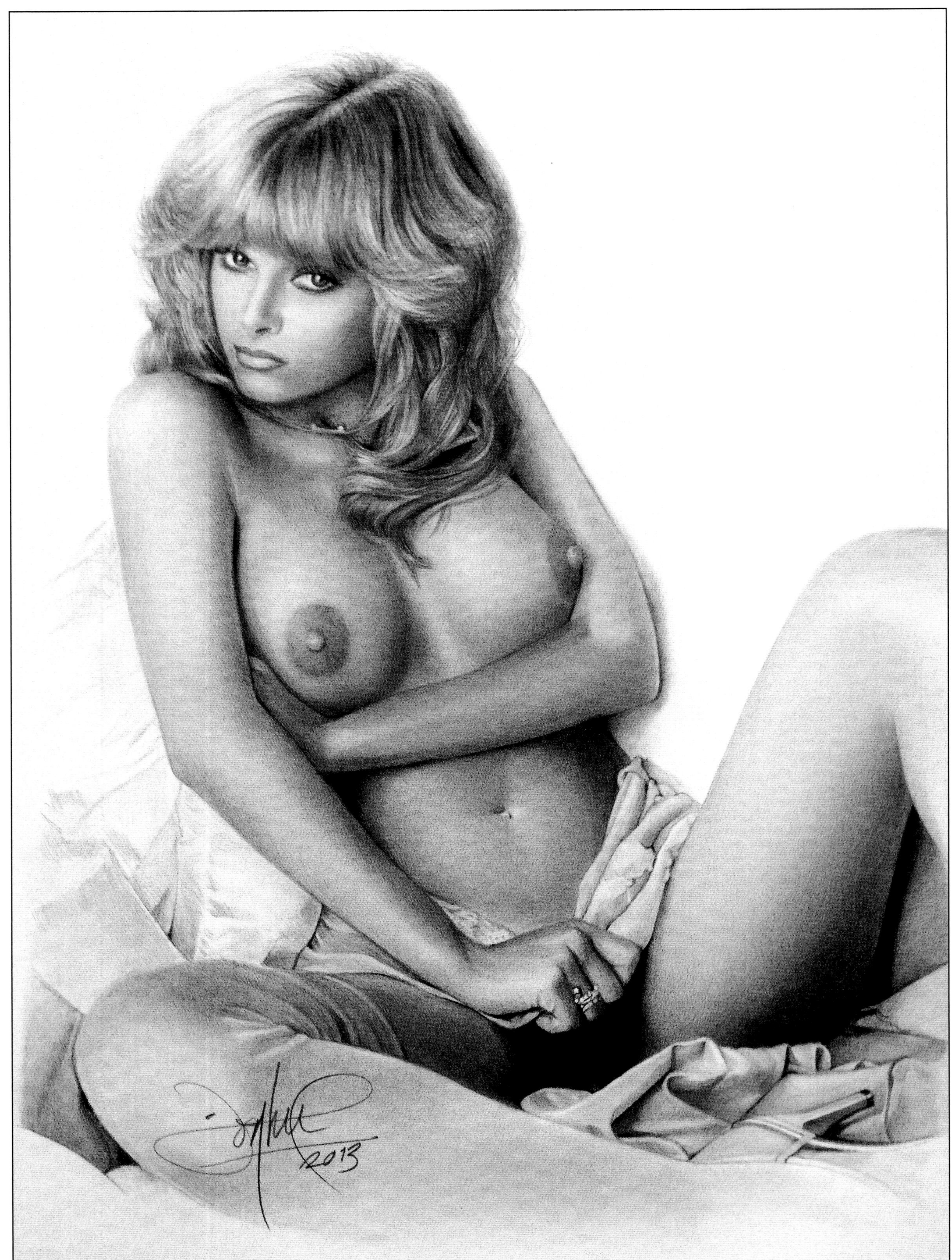

Santo Giorgio

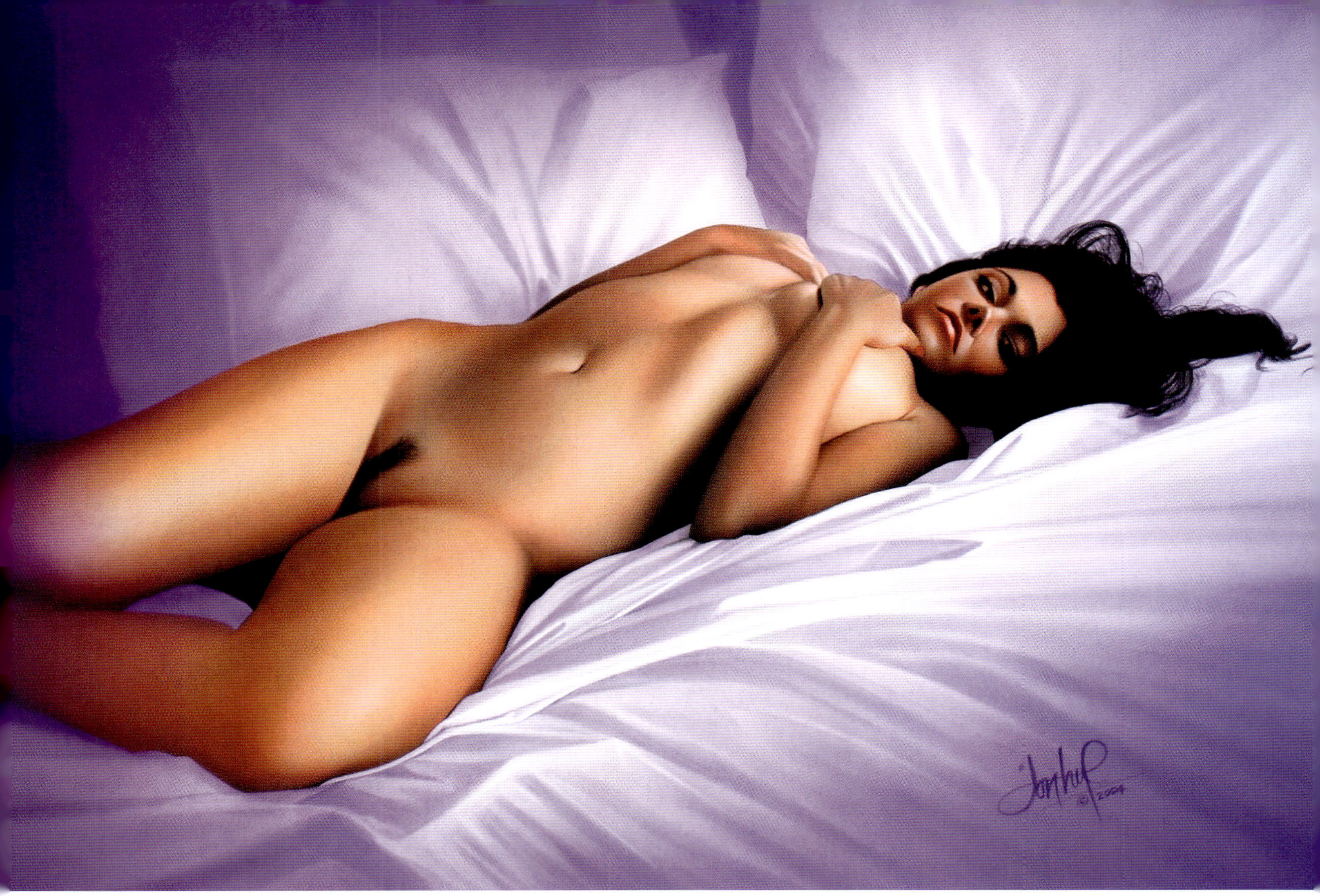

If You Belong To Me

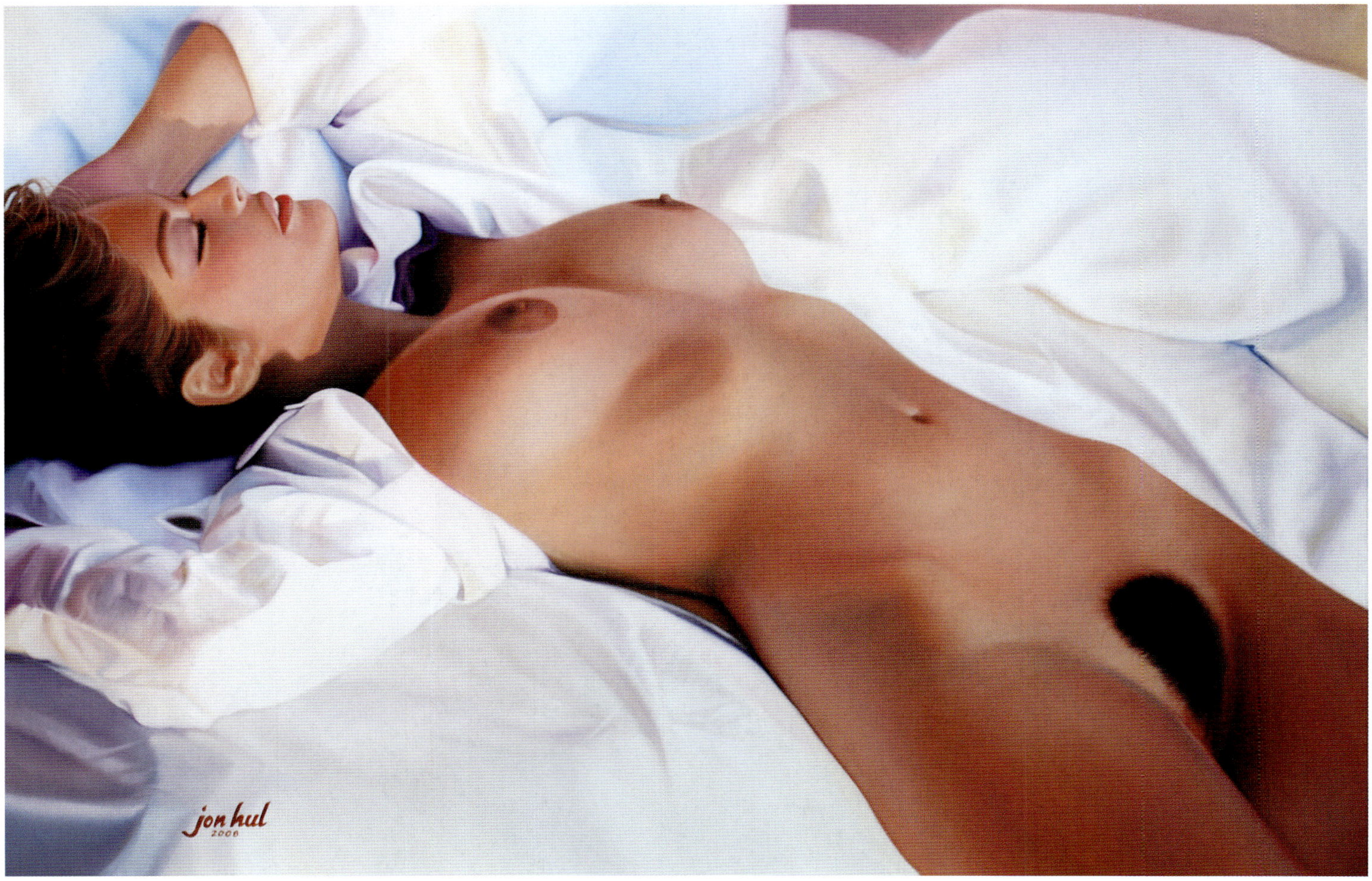

In A Dream

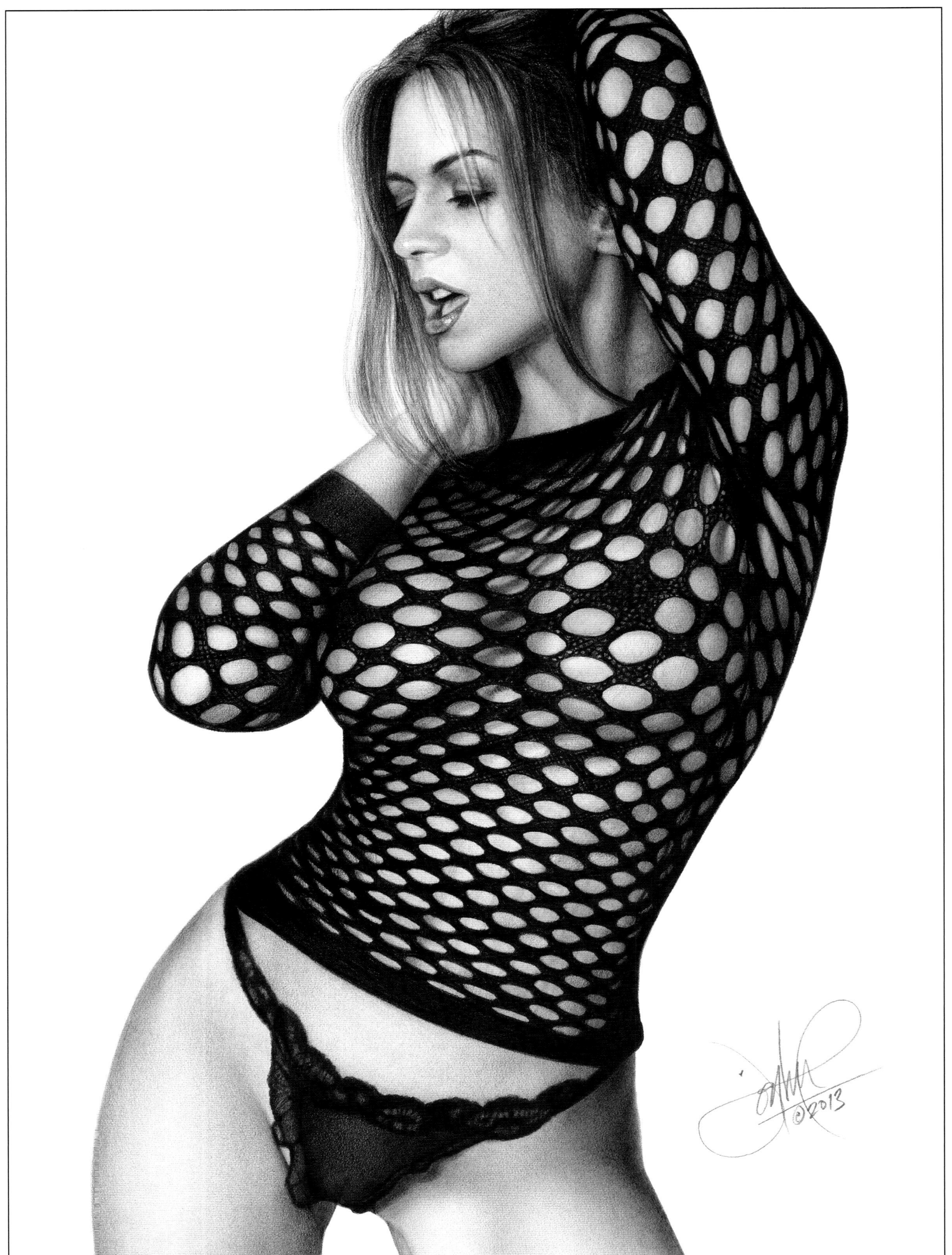

Feel The Move

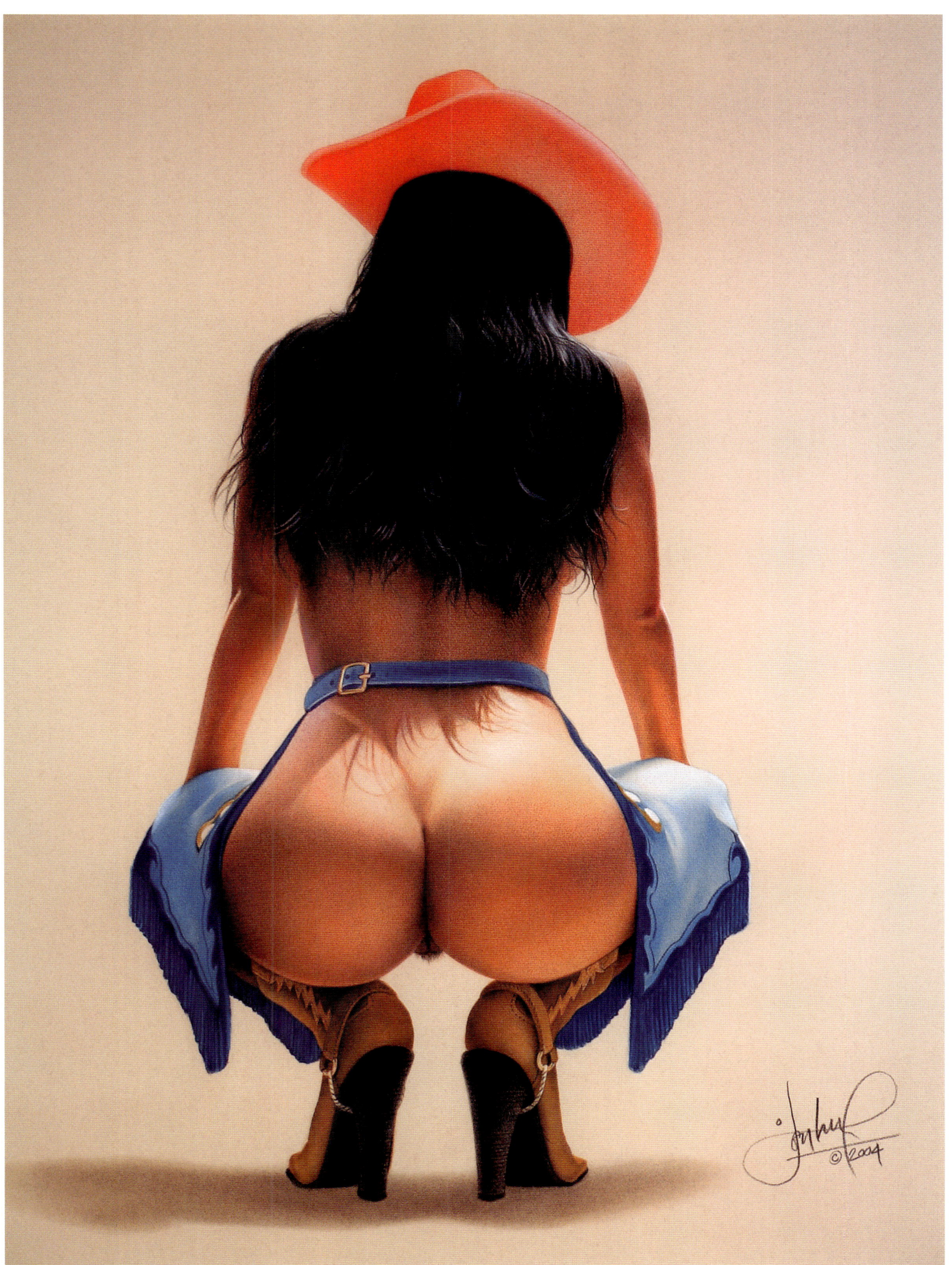

Nice Sweet Cheeks

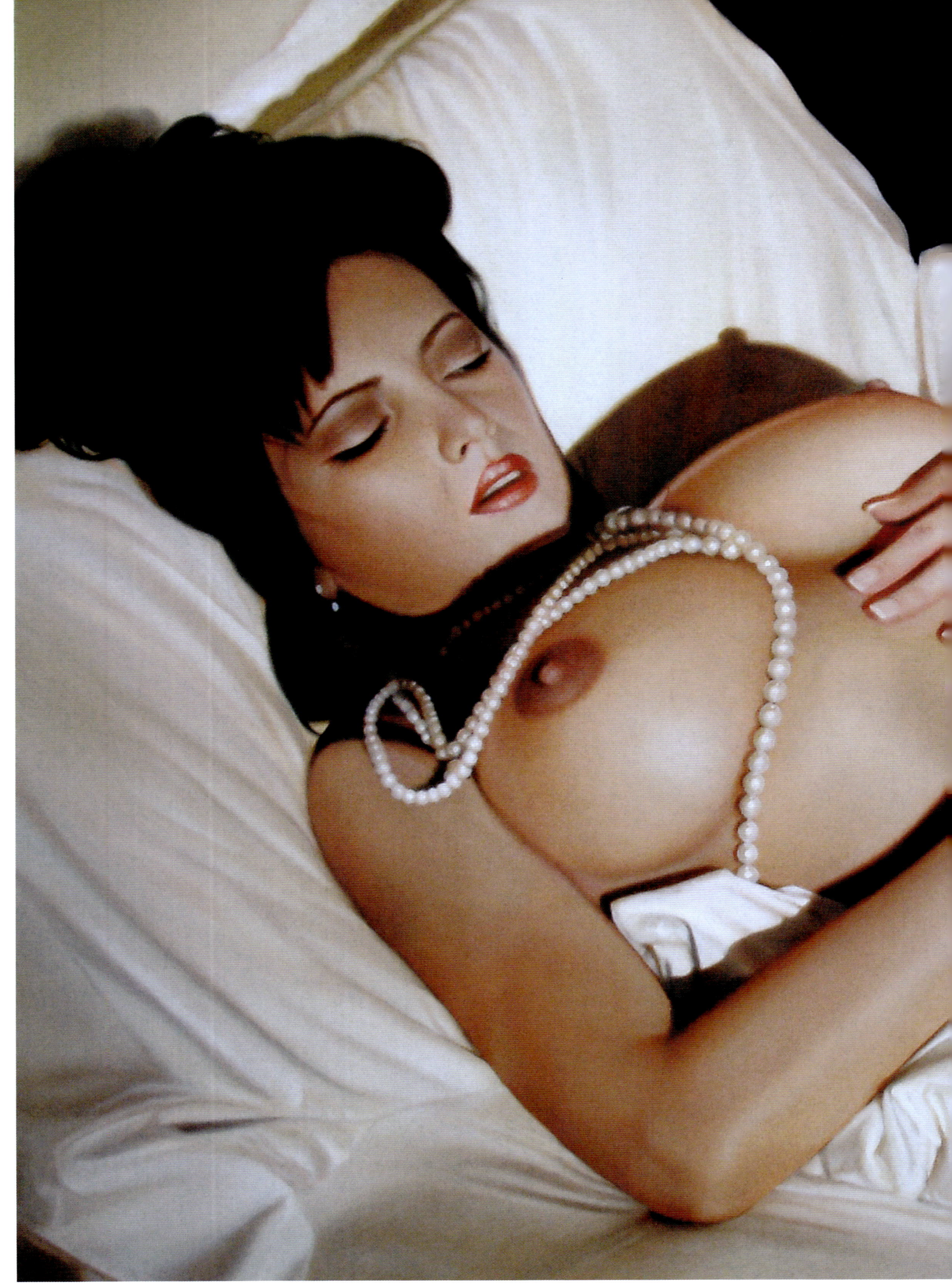

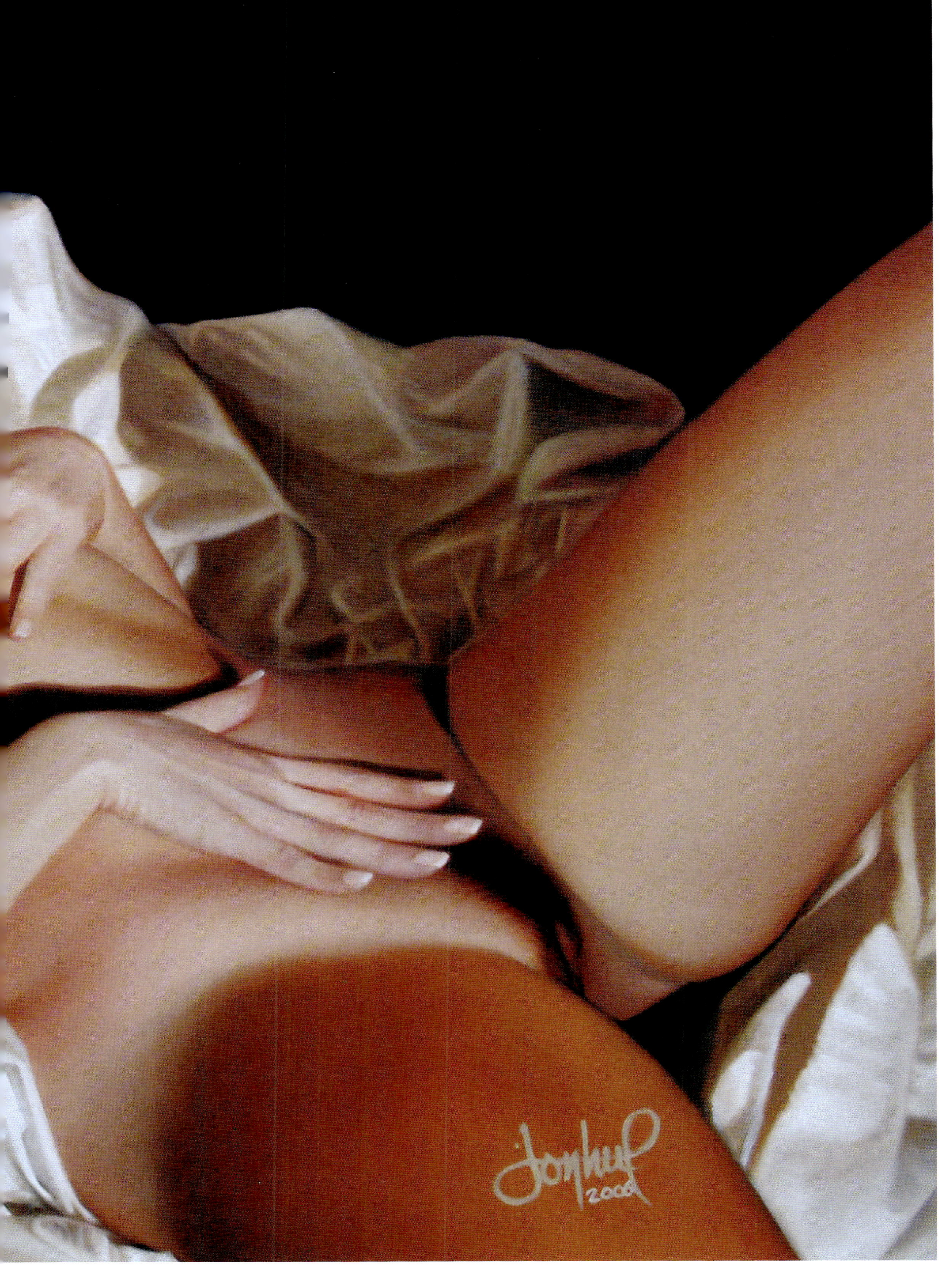

Bedtime Story

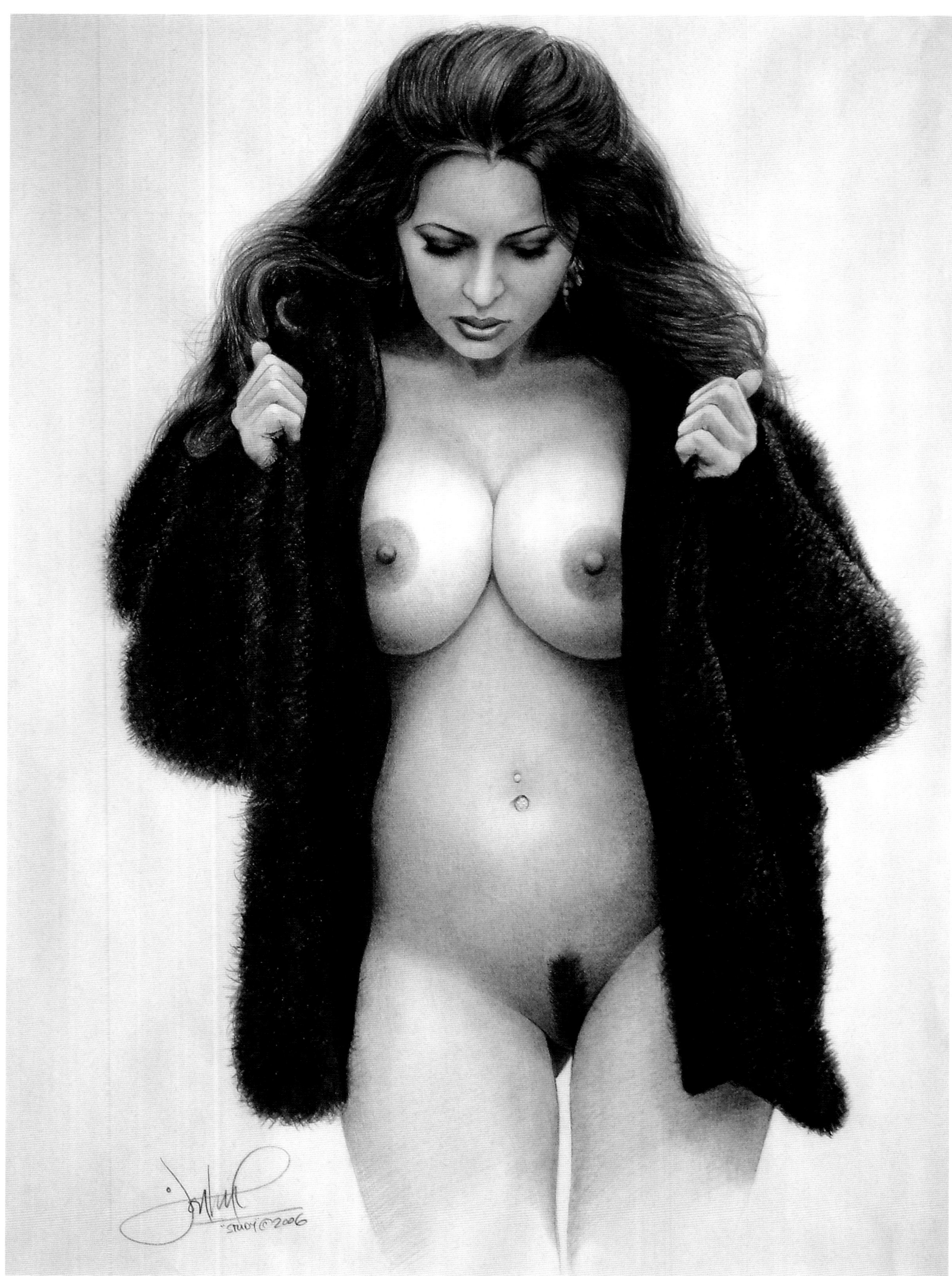

Resist Temptation - Pencil Study

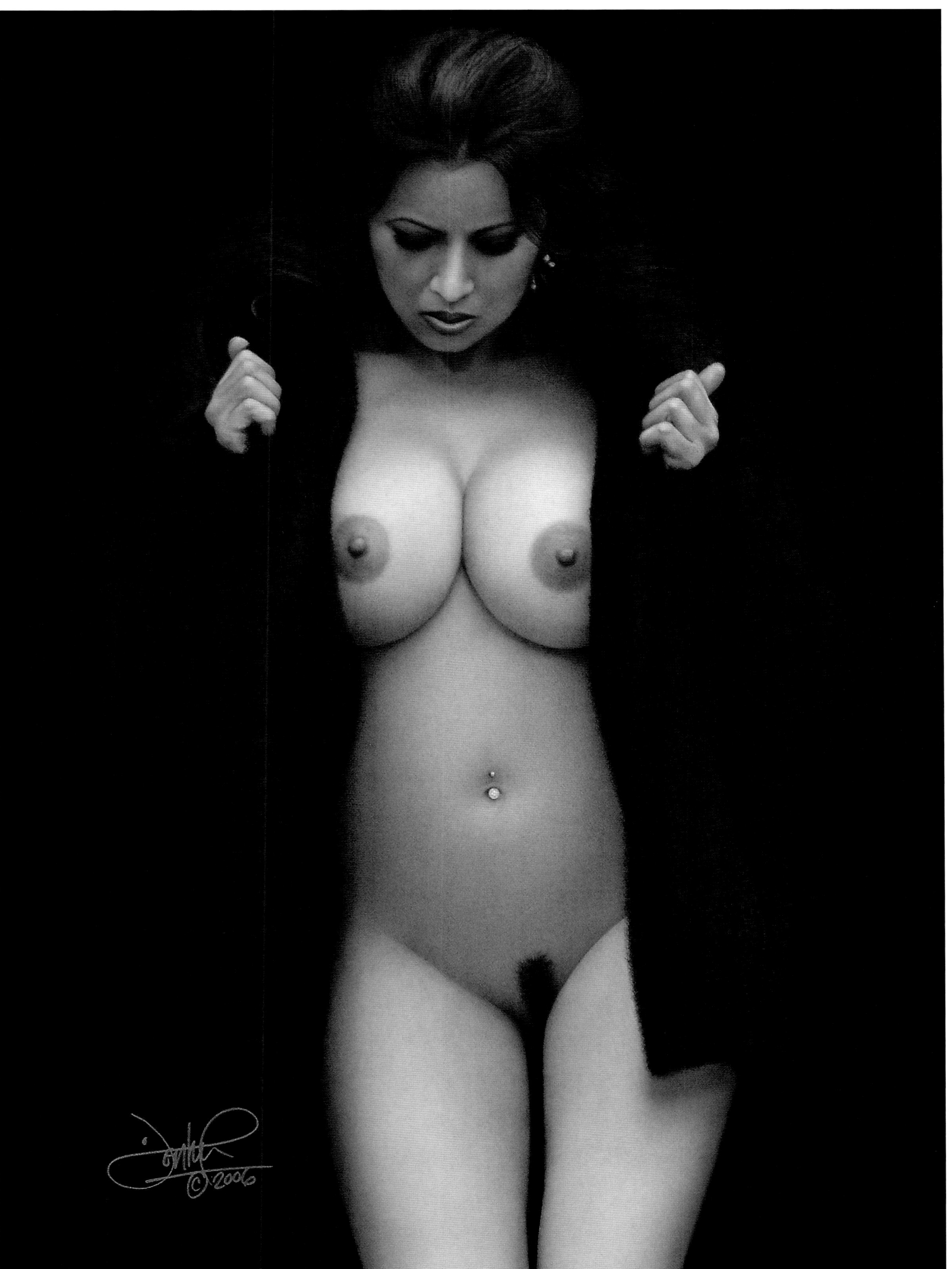

Resist Temptation

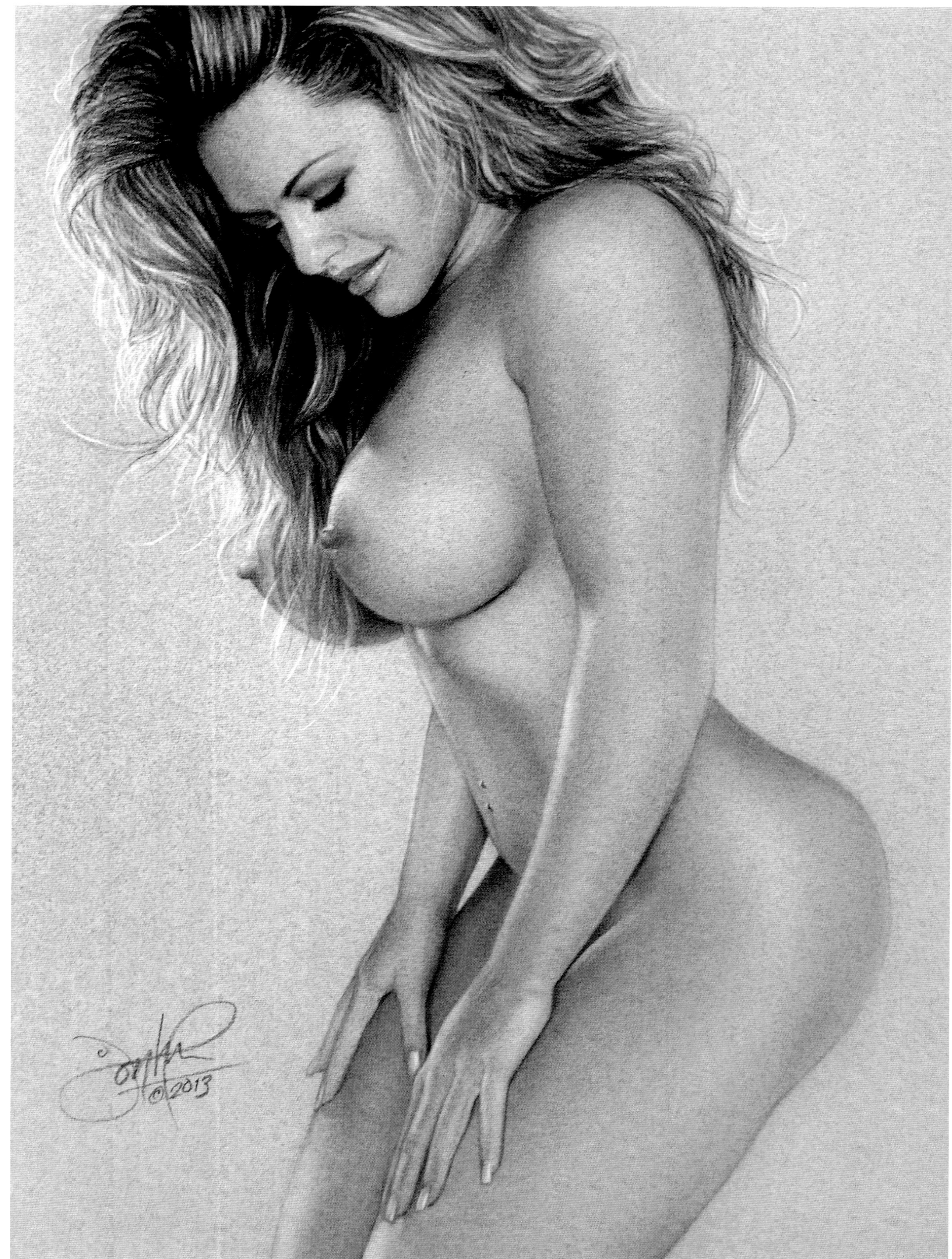

Points of Perfection

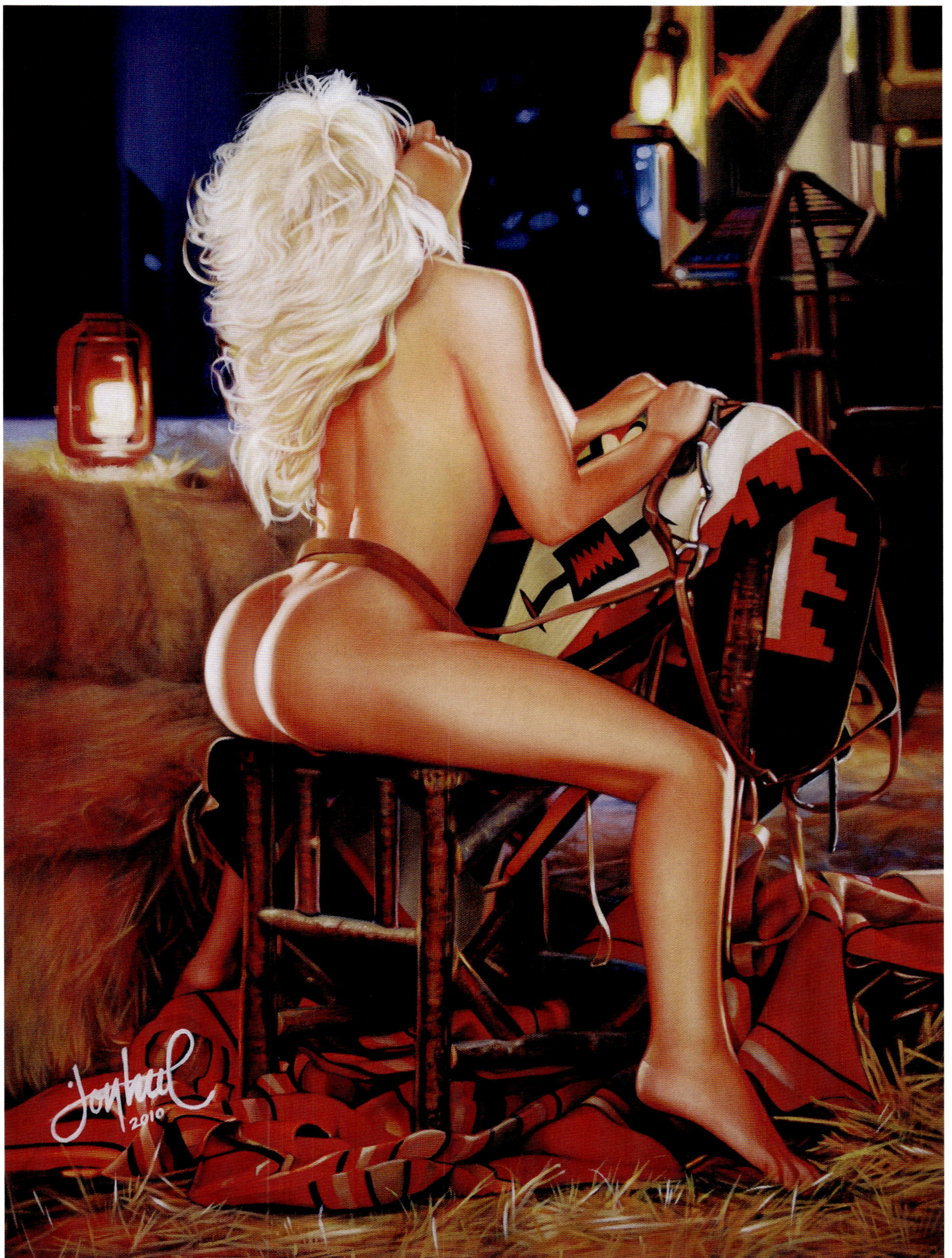

Midnight Ride

TRUE & TENDER

Up-close & personal with Jon Hul on the creation of an acrylic painting designed to showcase a perfect panty pull-down!

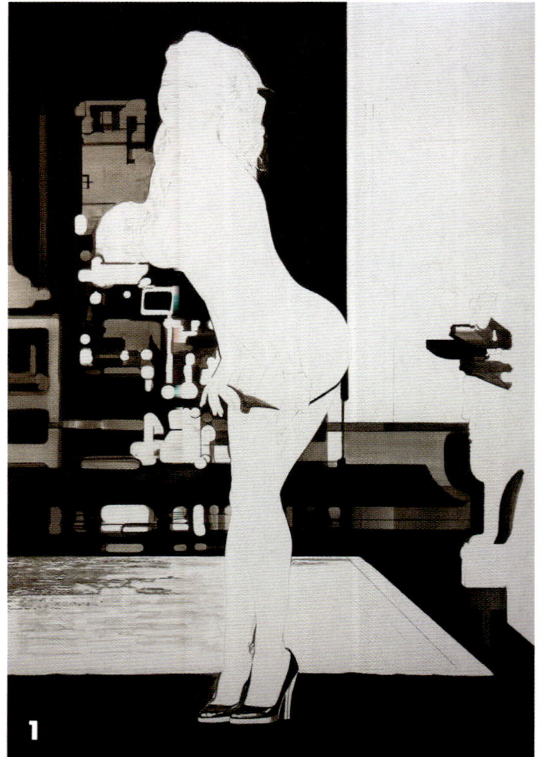
1

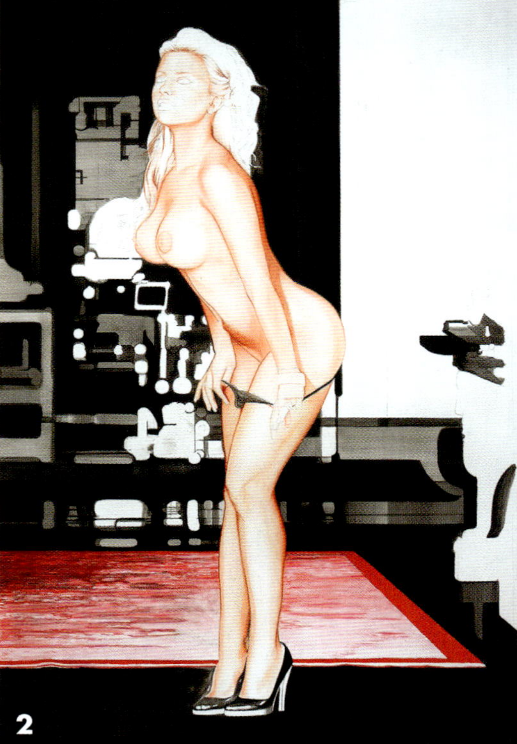
2

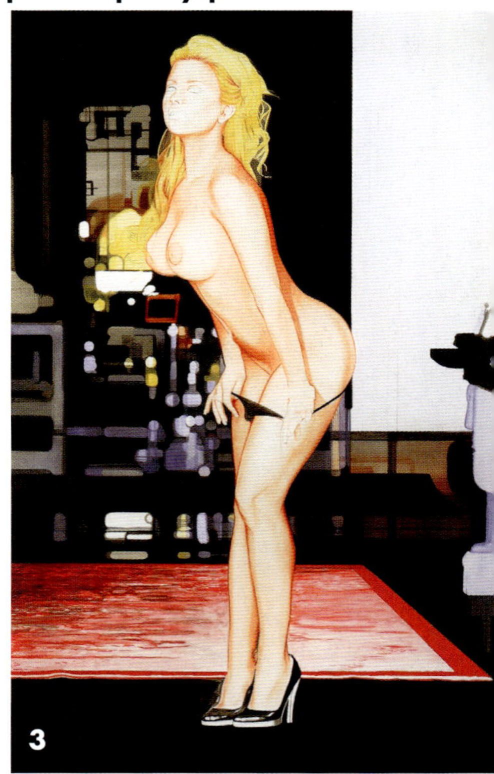
3

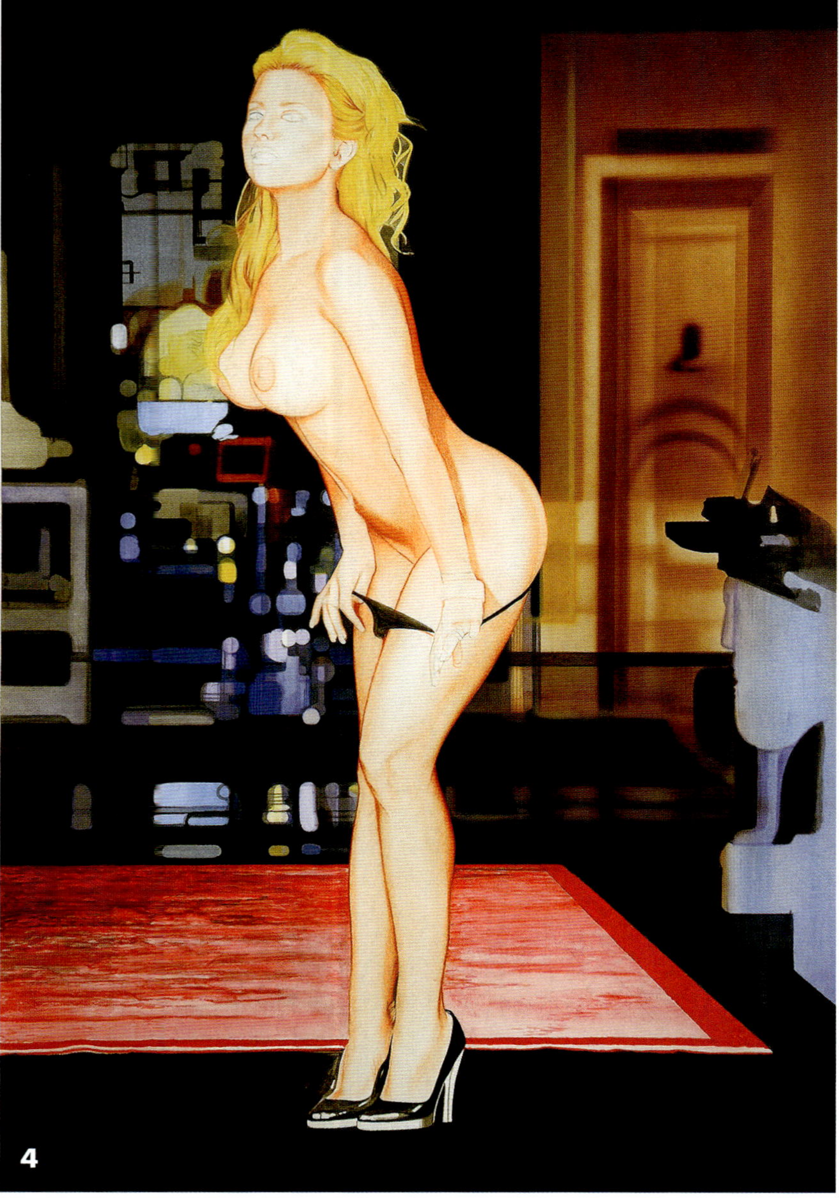
4

Step 1: A large illustration board (cold-press) was my choice of substrate used in rendering the new painting - "True & Tender", measuring 44" X 30". After completing the initial pencil layout, I began the "under painting" process by applying three different pigment colors (Ivory Black, Naphthol Crimson, and Burnt Sienna). These basic colors were applied by hand paint-brush paint technique. (Fine detail will be applied to the art during the latter portion of the paint process until completed.)

Step 2: By rendering the "under painting" process, the first transparent layer of Burnt Sienna pigment color was carefully brushed-in on the figurine, evenly. Then a second transparent layer (same color) was carefully applied, for mapping-out shadows and adding thick & thin lines to create contour of the body. Naphthol Crimson was the second pigment color application applied by dry brush (transparently), overlapping the outer edges of the figurine, and then overlapping (again) the initial black/gray half tones, giving me the opportunity to "sketch in" and simulate the texture of the carpet (and a bit of the background too). Please note: At this stage of the painting, my paint application is very basic, very essential and (most important) is "the" foundation of the work, period.

Step 3: Still using the hand paint-brush technique, a transparent layer of Cadmium Yellow pigment color was carefully applied evenly to the hair area of the figurine, and into different area's of the painting as well. I then added a transparent layer of Cobalt Blue pigment color to the background obstacles and enhance background color depth. And in some of the minimal area's of the background (where needed) I also applied and incorporated some small amounts of Cobalt Green pigment color to blend the transition of Cadmium Yellow to cobalt blue, adequately.

Step 4: I re-applied another layer of Burnt Sienna to the background area's, allowing me to mark color contrast and values, thusly. Being somewhat satisfied with the results of the amount of paint layers applied (from that point on), I then converted to the airbrush tool and applied light paint strokes (whisk's) to soften certain area's of the background, creating the "depth" within the piece.

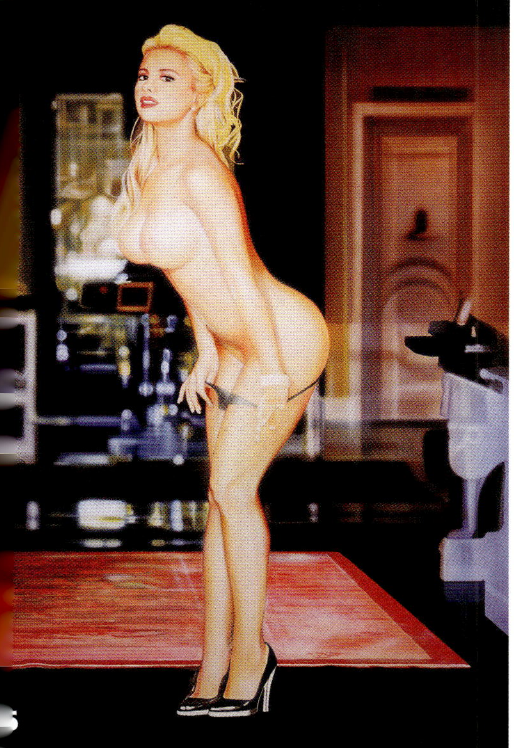

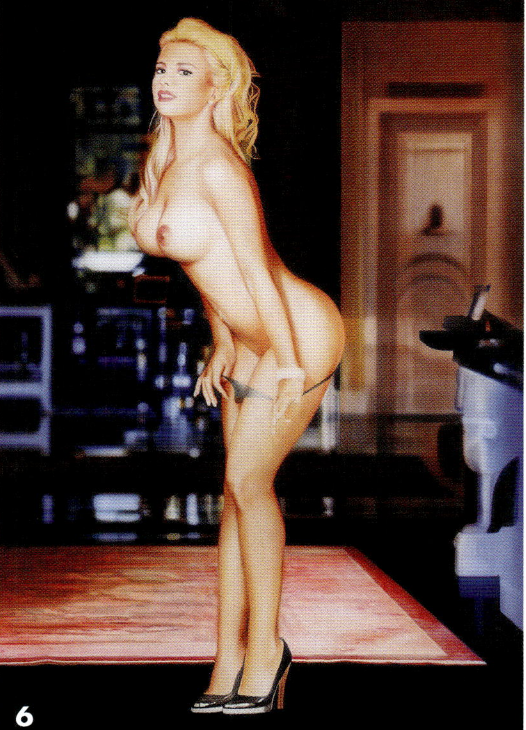

6

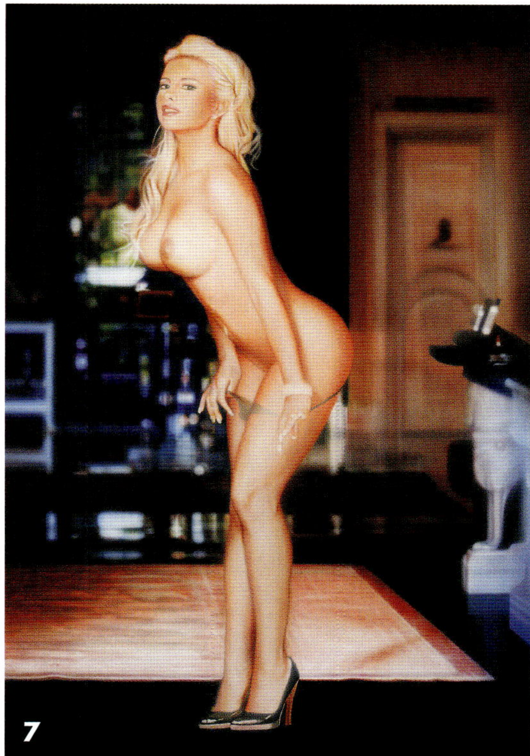

7

ep 5: From this point on I proceeded to focus the background area's first. I continued to ply a layer of Cobalt Blue pigment color by e of the airbrush tool application, applying en delicate strokes. During this process, several otle layers of pigment are applied to help eate and elevate the color intensity I wanted to satisfaction. Thus giving the "photo realism" usion appearance, effectively.

ep 6: At this stage of the work, I begin to pay ose attention to creating the "out of focus / urred" effect. To achieve that appearance, I had "think" my way through the process from its rly stages (one step up from the under painting vel) into the enhancing stages. Lot's of work volved into rendering the background, not an sy task to do. (Speaking in technical terms) total ncentration is the focal point when applying any pigments within that area of the work. And turn, achieving the best results from all of the rd work and concentration put forth into it. Very warding!

ep 7: At this stage of the work, I applied small nount of a palletted white pigment (not pure) d began to soften area's of the figurine, not tending to create highlights but rather create a ft-subtle of the skin, resulting in an even paint oplication consistency of the entire figurine. And en honing in on the characteristics the female's cial features (eye's, cheeks, nose, mouth, chin, c.),onto other vital parts of the figure from head toe.

ep 8: Applied fine detail to the carpet and ooring area's surrounding the figurine (from ack to front, and vice versa). From start to finish y goal for this painting was to evoke an overall ense of realism to the image, as if you could walk into the room where she is standing and in her". That was my achievement for this work f art... I hope it was convincing...

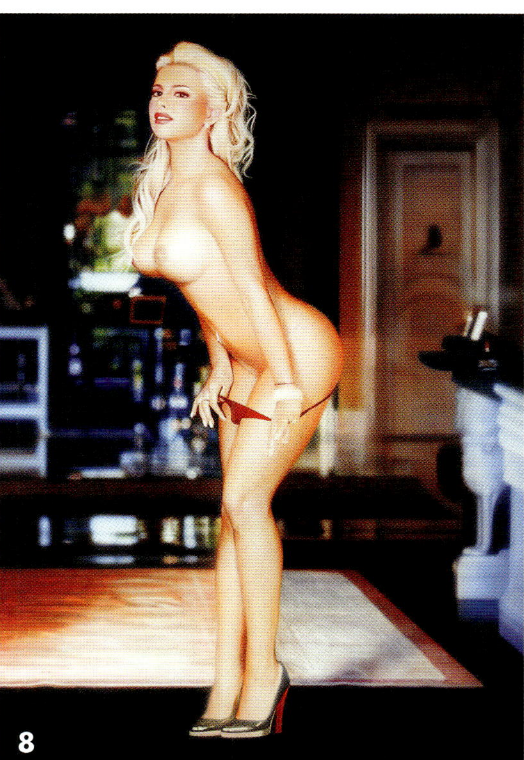

8

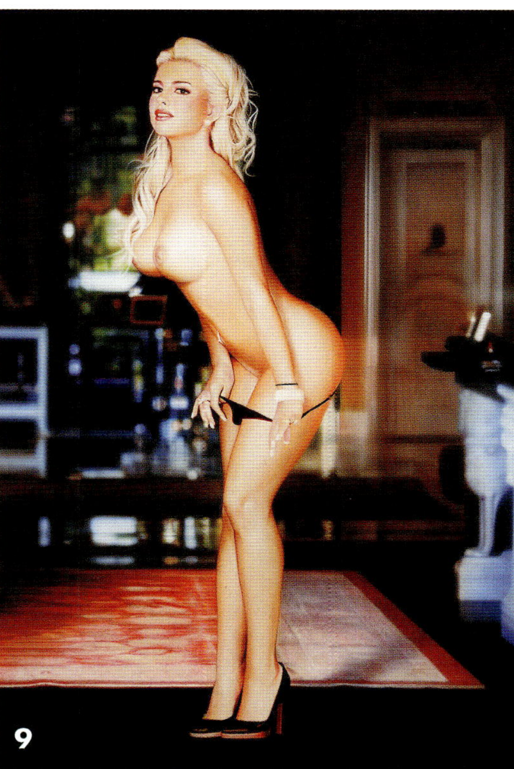

9

Step 9: Last but not least, in the final stage of the art I carefully re-applied Ultra-Marine Blue pigment color, then onto Ivory Black pigment for all dark area's of the painting, I used a combination of clear acetate specifically cut masks with a "free-hand" airbrush technique for just about every area rendered within the painting. Then applying fine diligent hand-brush work (again) to several area's from top to bottom until it was finally completed.

Following Page - Finale: More than five weeks were vested into the work, as I am very pleased with the out-come of it all. The gorgeous model portrayed in this painting is that of *Playboy Playmate* - ***Destiny Davis***. The work is entitled: "TRUE & TENDER". My pleasure to share the work with you all!

Enjoy, Jon Hul

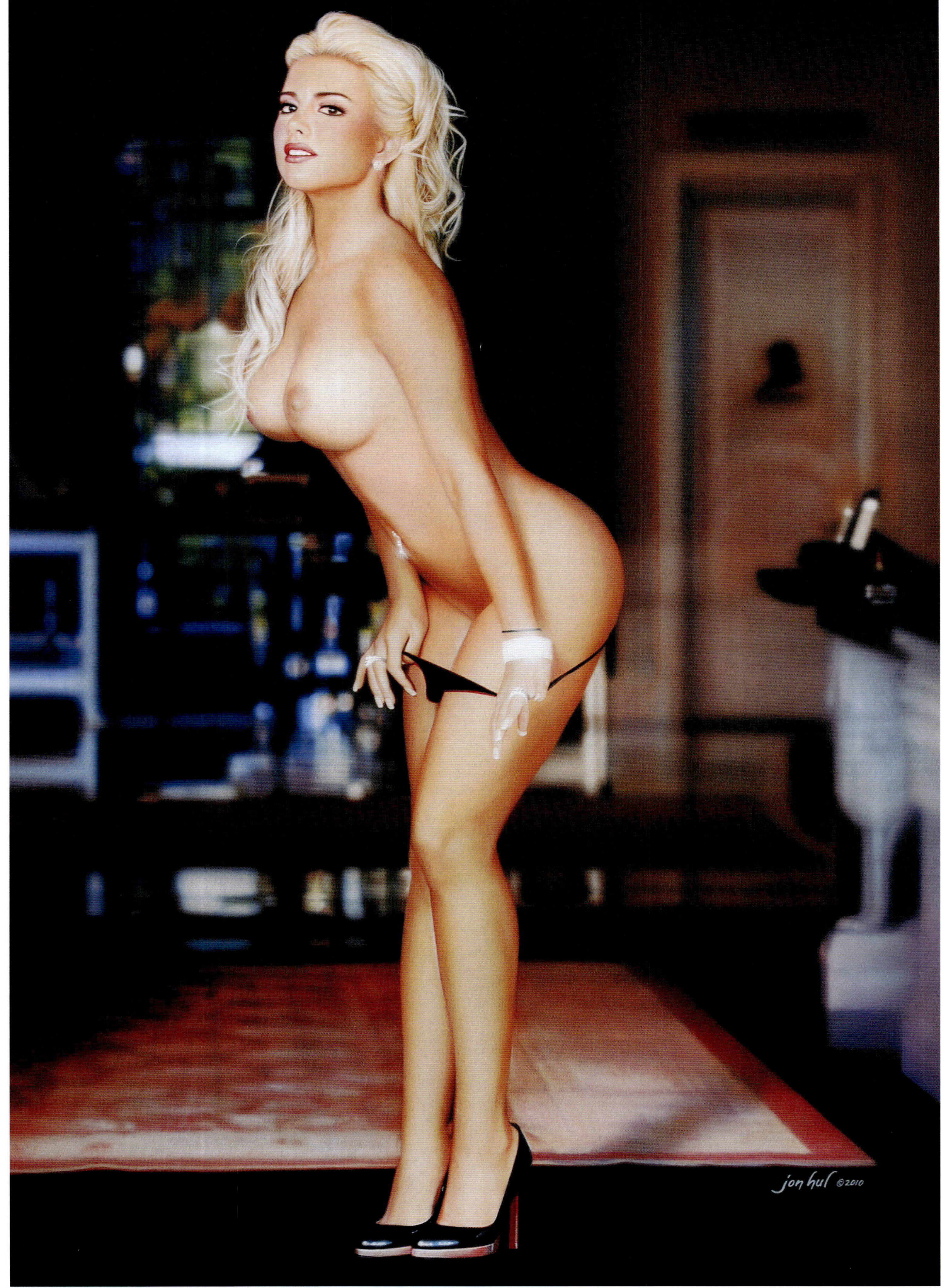

True & Tender